Kissing the Sky

Cristina Olsen

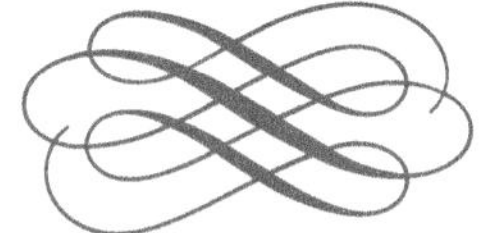

Kissing the Sky

Cristina Olsen

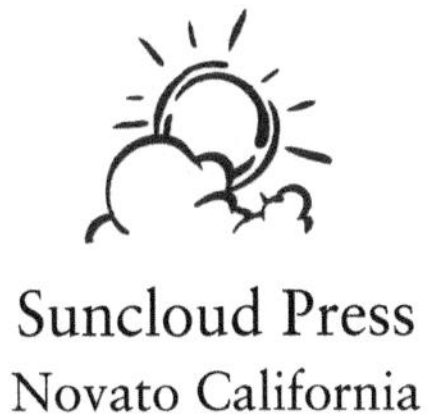

Suncloud Press
Novato California

Suncloud Press
P.O. Box 507
Novato, CA 94948-0507
www.cristinaolsen.com

Kissing the Sky
Library of Congress Control Number: 2014945594

I. Title: Kissing the Sky
II. ISBN: 978-0-9905328-2-8
1. Poems. 2. Prose Poems. 3. Photography

First Printing: January 2015

Book and cover design by Jim Shubin, www.BookAlchemist.net

Front and back cover photography: © Cristina Olsen
Back cover author photograph: © Dave Muñoz.

For Dave Muñoz (Haiku Dave), beloved husband and friend

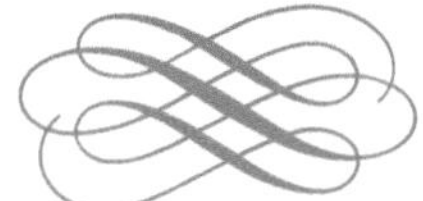

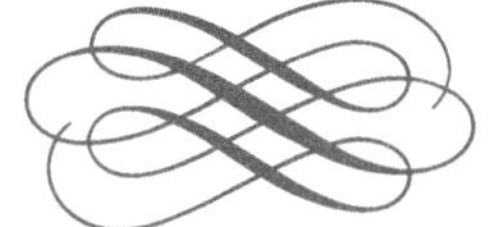

CONTENTS

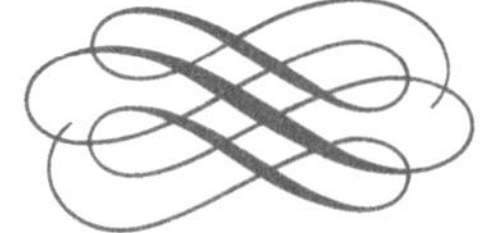

Author's Note

Kissing the Sky is an autobiography of the soul in poetic and visual form that begins with loss and loneliness, but soon transforms into love and an expansive freedom of the soul. From post-war London to the vast Pampas of Argentina, from Buenos Aires to the hills of Novato, California, I weave a meditative tapestry of poetry, poetic prose, and photography celebrating the beauty of nature and its power to transform pain into joy.

The book is divided into three parts, from finding light in the darkest hours, discovering love in all its guises, and reaching for the sky in blissful surrender. The accompanying photographs are not merely decorative. The way I take a photograph is the way I write a poem, circling the subject over and over again until the image says "take me!" I use the camera on my nature rambles to capture beauty, stalking prey like a hunter, every angle a joy to behold. And so every poem in this book evolves from a deep meditation with the image, and every image becomes a resonant backdrop that sends the poem flying—sometimes flying into unknown territory.

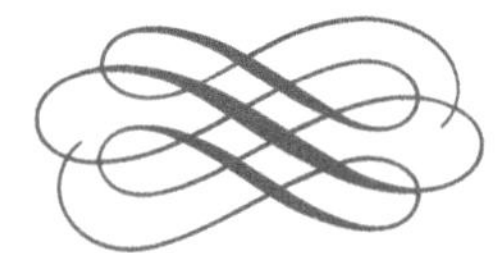

Part I
Lighting Up The Night

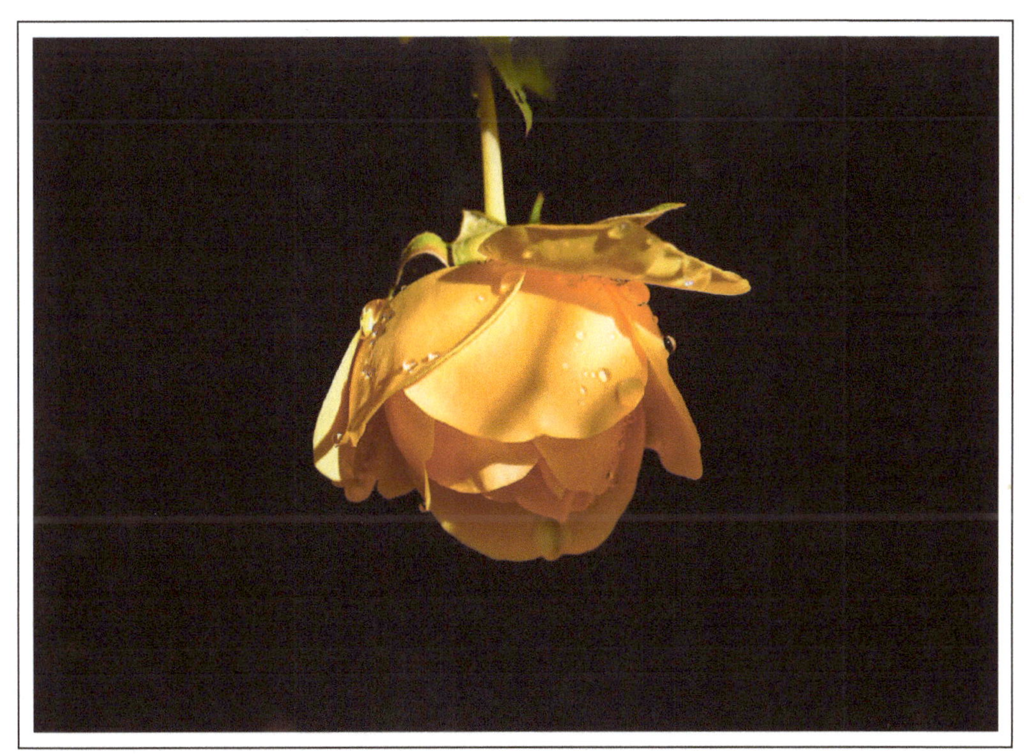

SOLAR WIND

Today I woke
with a far memory
stirring out of the dark.

I was a small child in a crib
wailing alone in the night,
when in he rushed, a solar wind
flooding the room with light,
lifting me up and holding me tight.

He was my father
for just a few years
a wind-swept ray from the spheres.

Twirling from room to room,
our laughter bubbled with heat
from pools of broiling glee,
following the jazzy beat
thumping out of the 78.

Or we pounded the piano keys,
hollering long forgotten ditties
to the war ghosts left behind
rustling the sagging blinds
in the crumbling London flat.

Ralph was his name,
a jazzy name,
a big fluffy dog name.

Then he was gone, so soon,
forever stuck in that gloom
between the night and day
of his alcohol daze,
glass in hand half full.

My first heartbreak,
solar wind across the night sky,
I will let you go now!

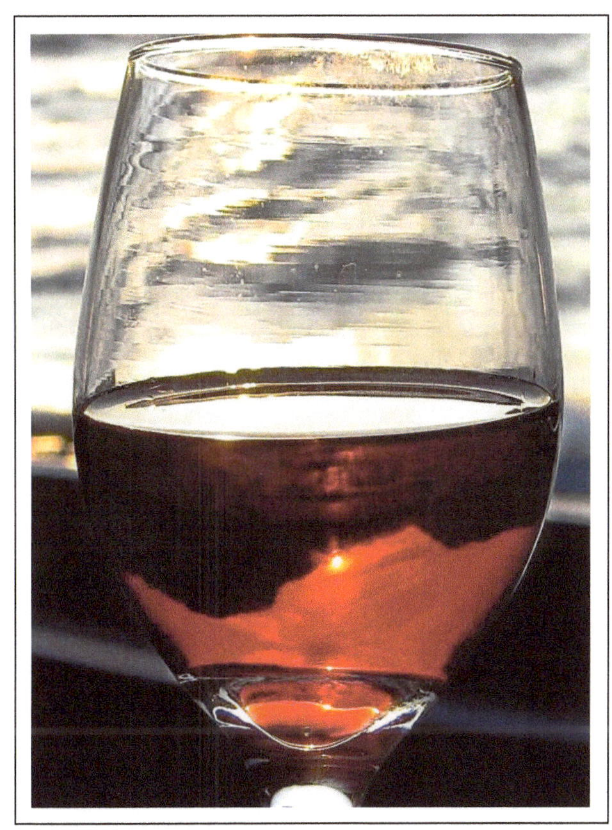

At The End Of Time

Grey on grey is what I recall of the London post-war years. Grey like the grey matter of my still small brain. Grey buildings, grey trees like skeletons looming out of grey mists, cobalt grey sky clamped down like a lid over an old metal pot.

I took my first steps slipping on grey slush along the footpaths of these end times, gripping the hand that grazed my cheek as I struggled to stay upright.

And yet, even in these dark times of bread queues and empty store windows, a pearly grey dawn mingled with promises of light drifted down from somewhere beyond the frigid sky.

One day, sunrays breached the metal lid of the sky and kissed the frigid snow, beckoning children to gather around and build a snowman, my own pudgy hands slapping on the snowballs around the ever widening girth.

Buttons for eyes, a carrot for a nose, pipe shoved into a smirking mouth, plaid scarf draped around the broad neck, and a top hat for rank. And so we birthed the new man out of sparkles from heaven and the paraphernalia of the old world, ready to sing forth "Rule Britannia!" Some things never change.

Tea and crumpets awaited, and we all rushed in out of the cold, beckoned by fire-lit hearths and rousing tales of heroism in the glow of the orange light.

Many end-times have furrowed my brows since then, building up then crashing down. Yet I still see the snowman standing there, forever turned towards the ray of a rising sun behind the swelling of a cobalt-blue cloud.

The terrible beauty of all the dying and the living takes my breath away.

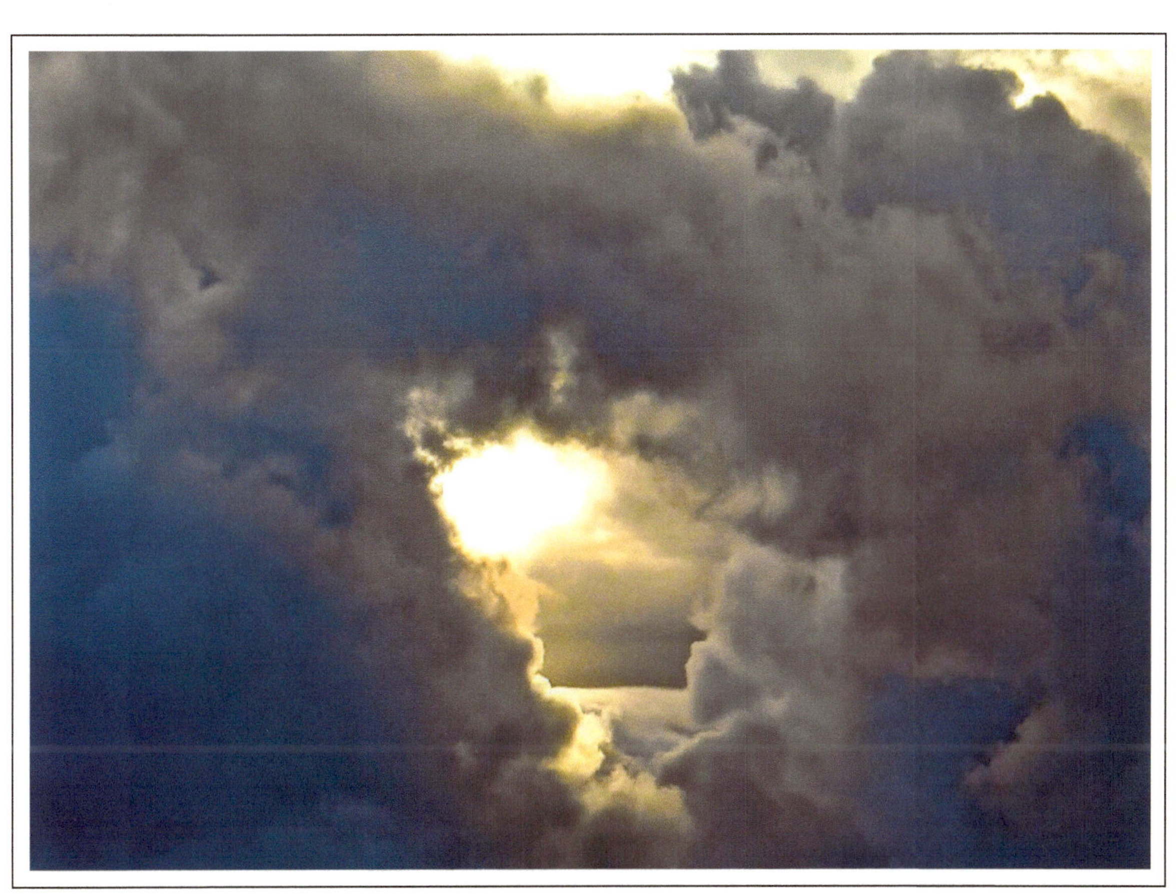

BEAUTY'S PASSING

In a time of Beauty
forests grazed by billowing clouds,
deserts alight like candles in the sun,
fields anointed by wending streams,
all these lay before my feet.

And yet here I now stand,
here in this sliver of time,
watching dark shapes
where gloom pervades
in harrowing fashion.

Wait! Stop! Whitewash the canvas!
I will dip my brush in a new vein.
Beauty shall not be vanquished
by the dark night of these times.
See the light in her womb how it blazes!

Lest you forget, I will paint
the feathers in her hair
and the hem of her gown
sweeping the dark ground
as she leaves traces of her passing.

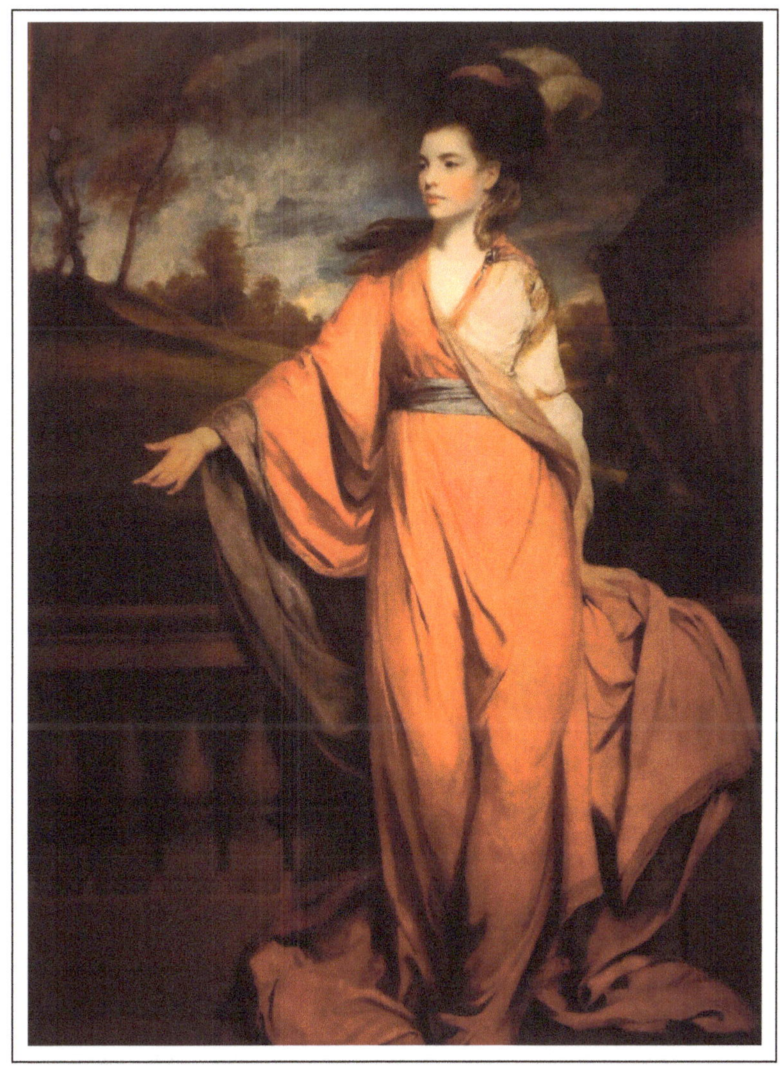

Lady Jane by Joshua Reynolds, © *Courtesy of the Huntington Art Collections, San Marino, California*

Vortex Of Light

As a child I roamed the Pampas of Argentina — a flat, shadowless land that dips into an endless horizon under the merciless canopy of the sky, where the sun glows incandescent, fanned by the pearled-green of sprouting wheat, soon to be transformed into carpets of gold paving the way for the final blaze scorching the earth to ashen brown.

On that flat expanse of land, light overseas all minutia of the fields: fence-posts and wildflowers, birds and field-mice, windmills and puddles, barns and laborers, gauchos herding cattle and sheep — all surfaces awash with a light that masks the deeper and darker core of things.

As a child, the limitless expanse lay bare before my feet, stretched out towards that distance where land and sky kiss, where touch is more real than sight, the breeze a loving caress on the cheek, the wind a passionate embrace of an invisible deity.

Now in the prime of my life, far from the land of my birth, I see the light-filled Pampa as but the lustrous veil of something deeper.

I close my eyes, the breeze fans my skin. Beyond the far horizon a solar wind speeds towards me. Fearless, I will breathe in deeply that wind that is the deep vortex of all lights.

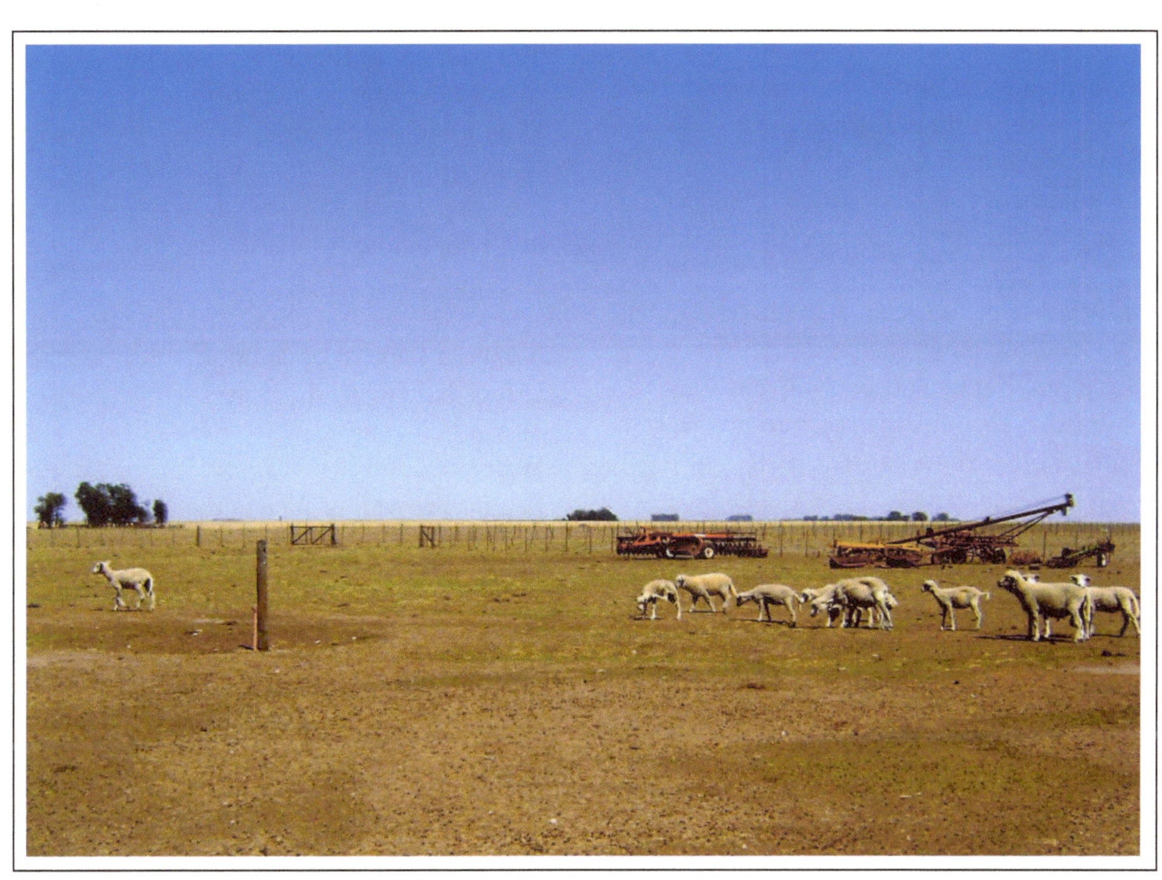

THE OPEN BOOK

I am an open book
pouring myself out in rivers of print
from another time, another place.
Decades of underground torrents
of ancient springs dampened by silence
from another time, another place.

Mother said, "we keep it to ourselves,
we swallow down the pain."
I ran and hid behind bramble bushes,
slipped in through the crack in my heart
into another time, another place.

The Oneness of India
drifting down the Ganges
couldn't draw me out.
The Tao of China tried.
Arctic shamans froze in the tundra.
Zen monks flickered on and off
across the empty canvas.

The prophet of the Now came too,
then vanished into the Not Now.
Even joyful Jesus came,
with tambourines and wine,
then the church squashed him
like a fly before my eyes.
I shudder still.

No, now I am an open book,
letters dancing to the beat
of just being alive.
Hear the noise?
Behind the wail of pain is the shout of joy.

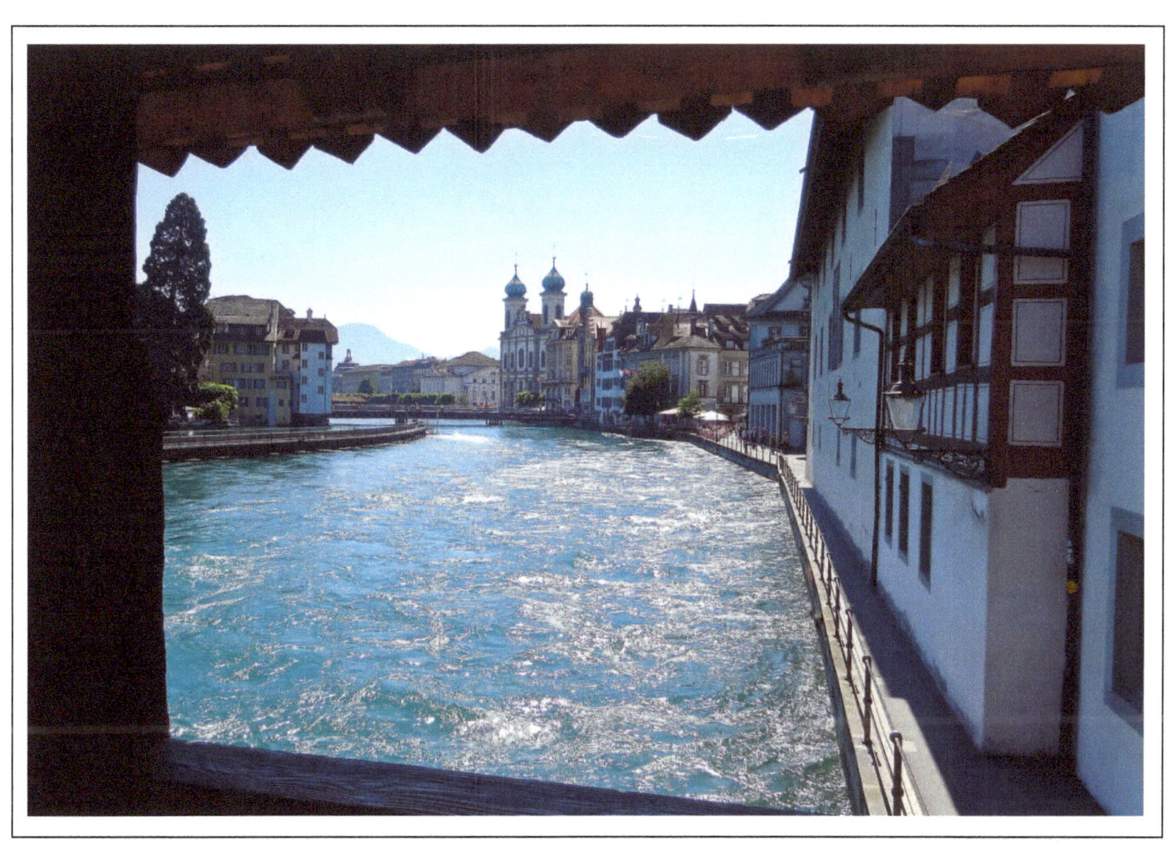

LITTLE MUTTER

Little Mutter was her name,
scrappy dog of many scars.
She lay with me that first night,
trembling in my arms with fright.

Something in my heart broke loose,
blossomed in the bonding salve,
high romping in spirit flights
in the garden of delights.

Then life took a sudden turn,
ships signaling a new land.
Lay her down in sackcloth brown,
and sailed half the world around.

Bones now lie in roots entwined,
feeding branches to the skies,
memos sent on ocean swells:
"all is well, friend, all is well."

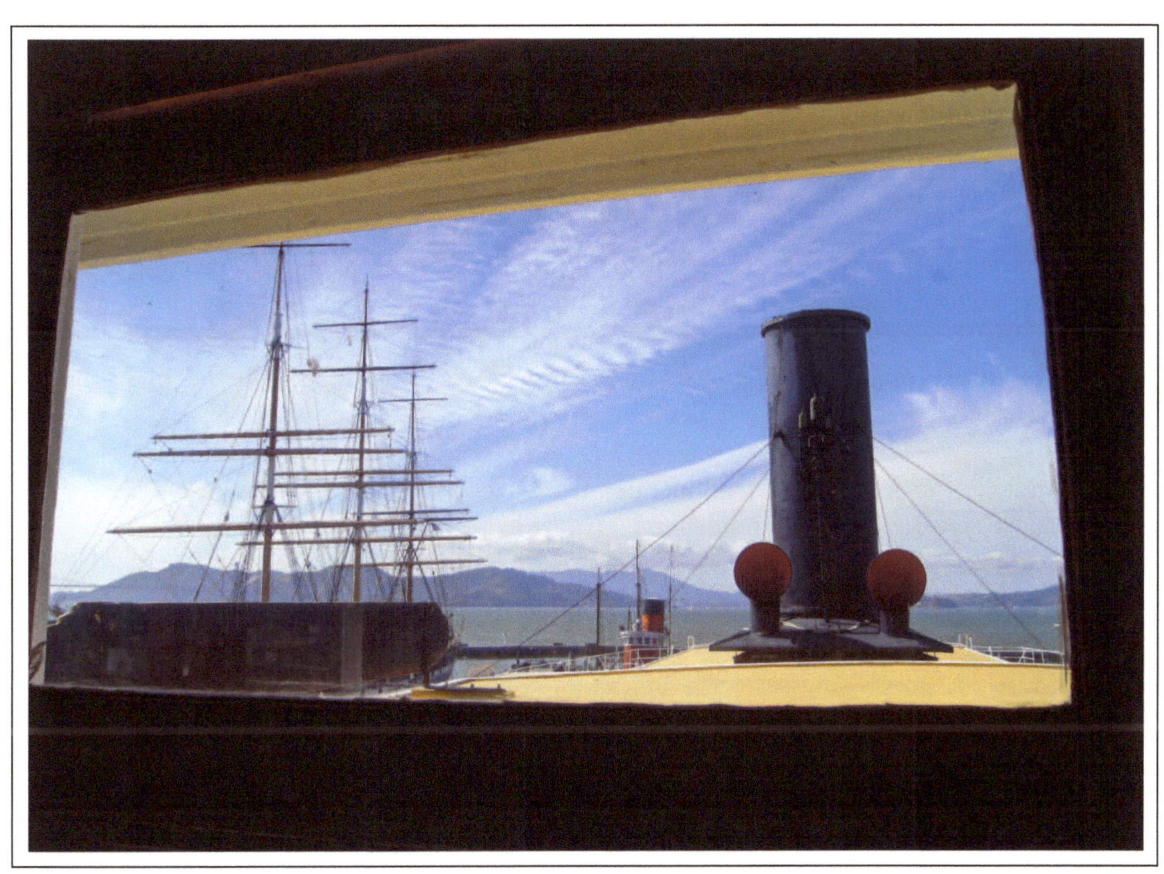

THE LUMINOUS UNSEEN

I stand at the lake's edge, the sun setting beyond the darkness in which we live, just enough light to see the shocking war dance between the light and the dark.

I stand here drenched by the waning light, perplexed that I can still feel joy even as the darkness presses in.

Who is that mystic warrior standing firm with plumed lancet held aloft, piercing the looming dark with such aplomb?

After all things on earth have poured out their last breath, she lunges forth, cracks the darkness and lets the luminous unseen pour in.

I stand here now in the dark, smiling, alighted by the inpouring of the unseen. Sunlight wounds the eye, but the luminous unseen transforms the eye into luminous being.

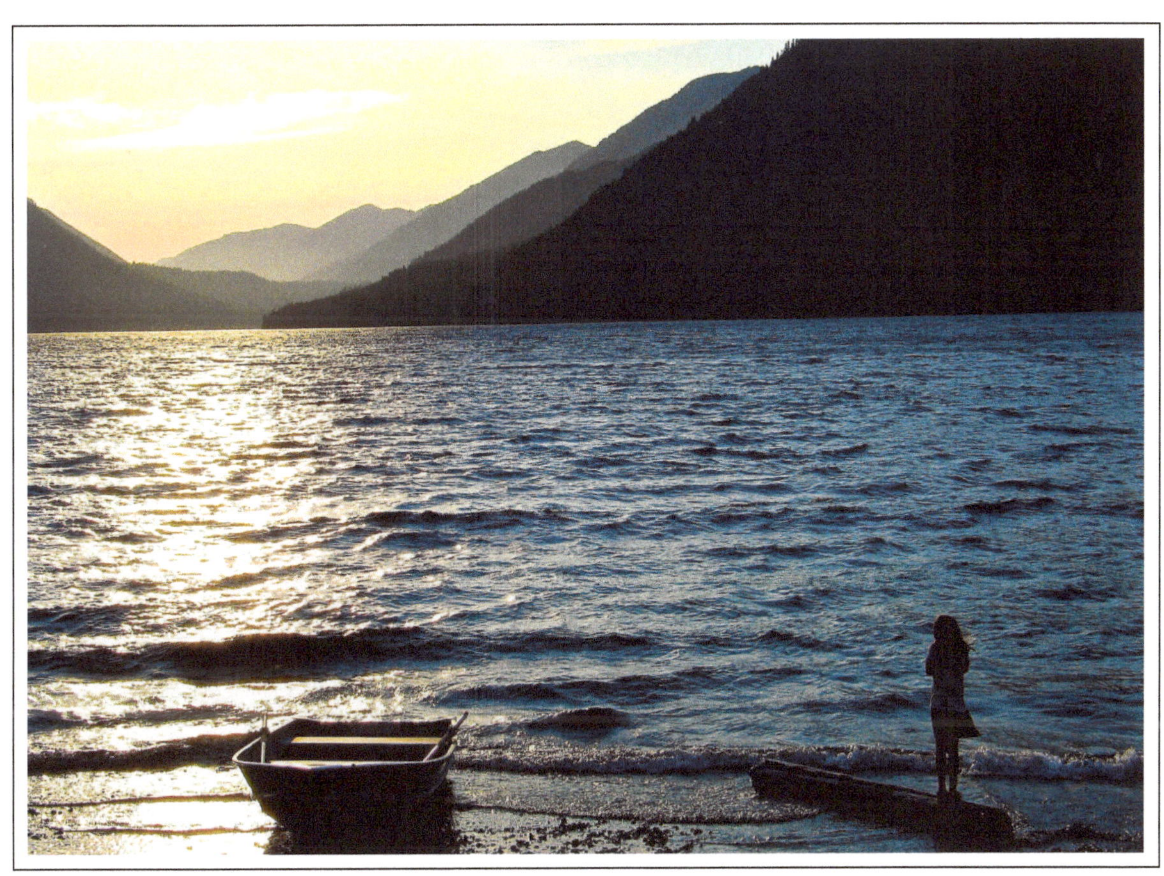

Dark Night and Sun Rise

Dark Night and Sun Rise
came from distant lands,
a Doberman and a Dingo,
prowling around in limbo.

Life was rough then,
girl roaming hippie parks
astride a lover's Harley bike,
world of hard rock and other highs.

Took to the hills when I could,
canine friends leading the way
to where frontier airs
filled my lungs with sun flares.

Freedom alone is a burning fire,
but Dark Night and Sun Rise
taught me to love in mystic guise,
kissing the sun with my eyes.

I find them now on higher ground
looking ahead to regions wild
where I too now stand at night
shoulders draped in rays of light.

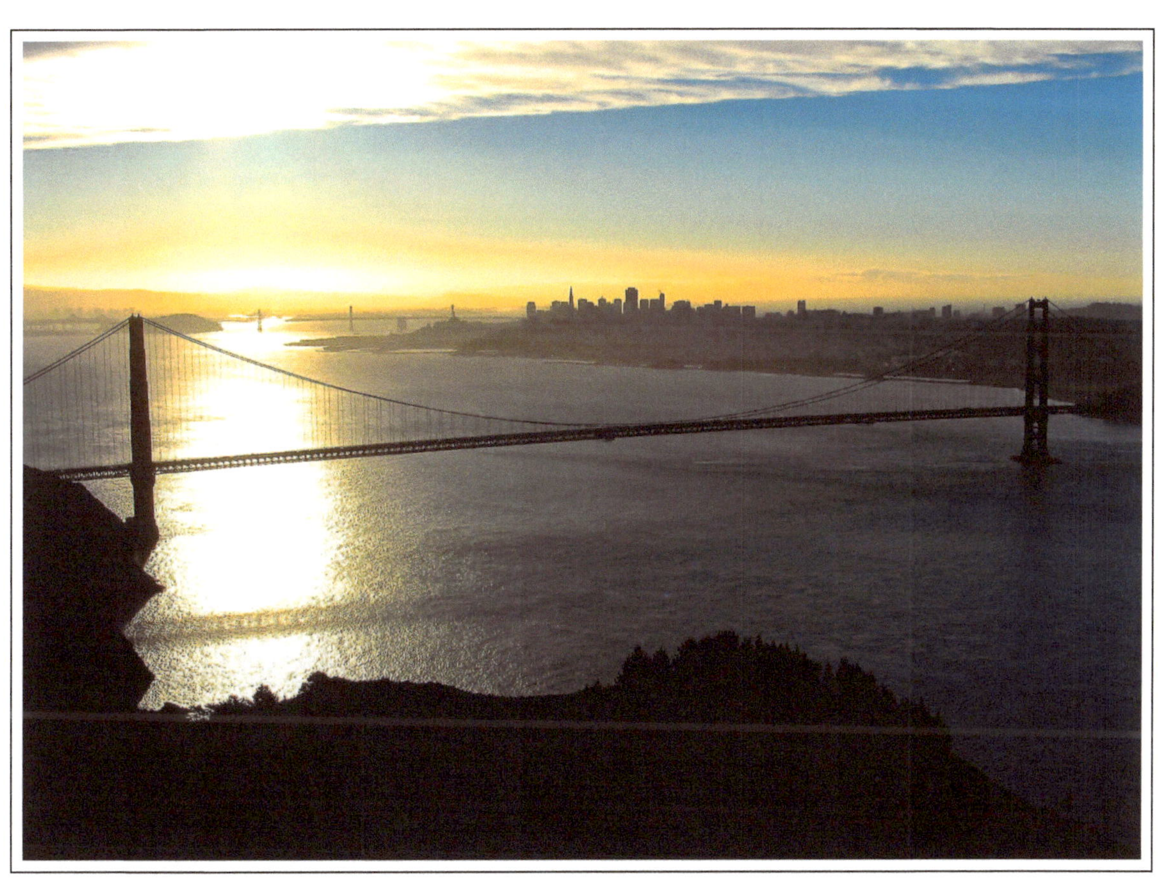

MAN ON A BIKE
(In Memoriam)

He blew in
like the desert wind
flame in flight
this was he

Still
he watered my plants
from deep reserves of life

This was he
colored like an autumn rose
a man aglow
with glistening chrome

Gone
on wings of desire
flaming chariot across the universe

Still
rain descends
washes clean the pain
this is he returning

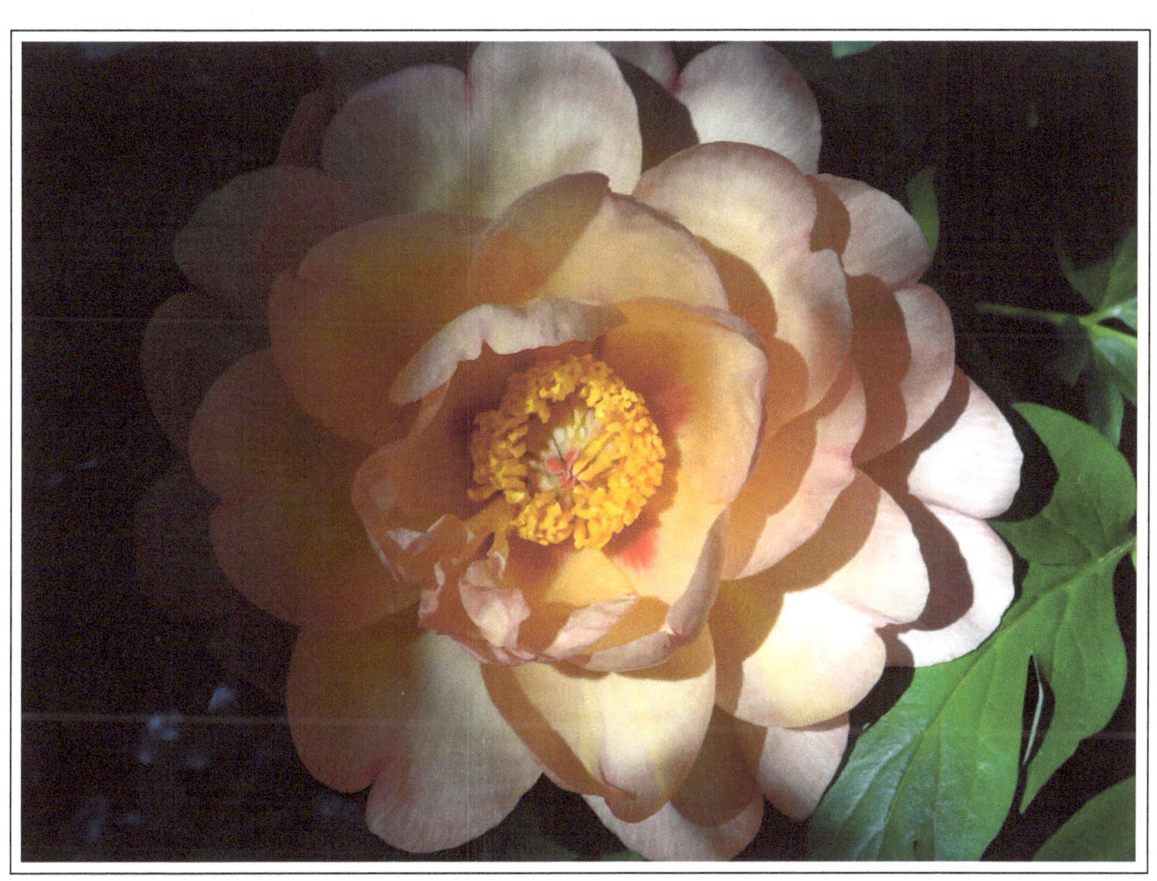

NOSTALGIA

I stand on the crest of nostalgia, the seascape stretched below. The fog rolls back and I see the lived and not yet lived, one fitting into the other in seamless symmetry.

I stand on the crest of nostalgia, sunrays trumpeting a call to gather up the threads and descend where the ocean bleeds into the land.

I walk along the wind-swept beach to where my future waits, as waves erase all traces of my passing, a ghostly sail on the horizon.

Tides draw all the lived and not yet lived down into ocean nurseries. Still, nostalgia will raise me up again to ascend the pilgrim's path to where new life flows into the passing of the old.

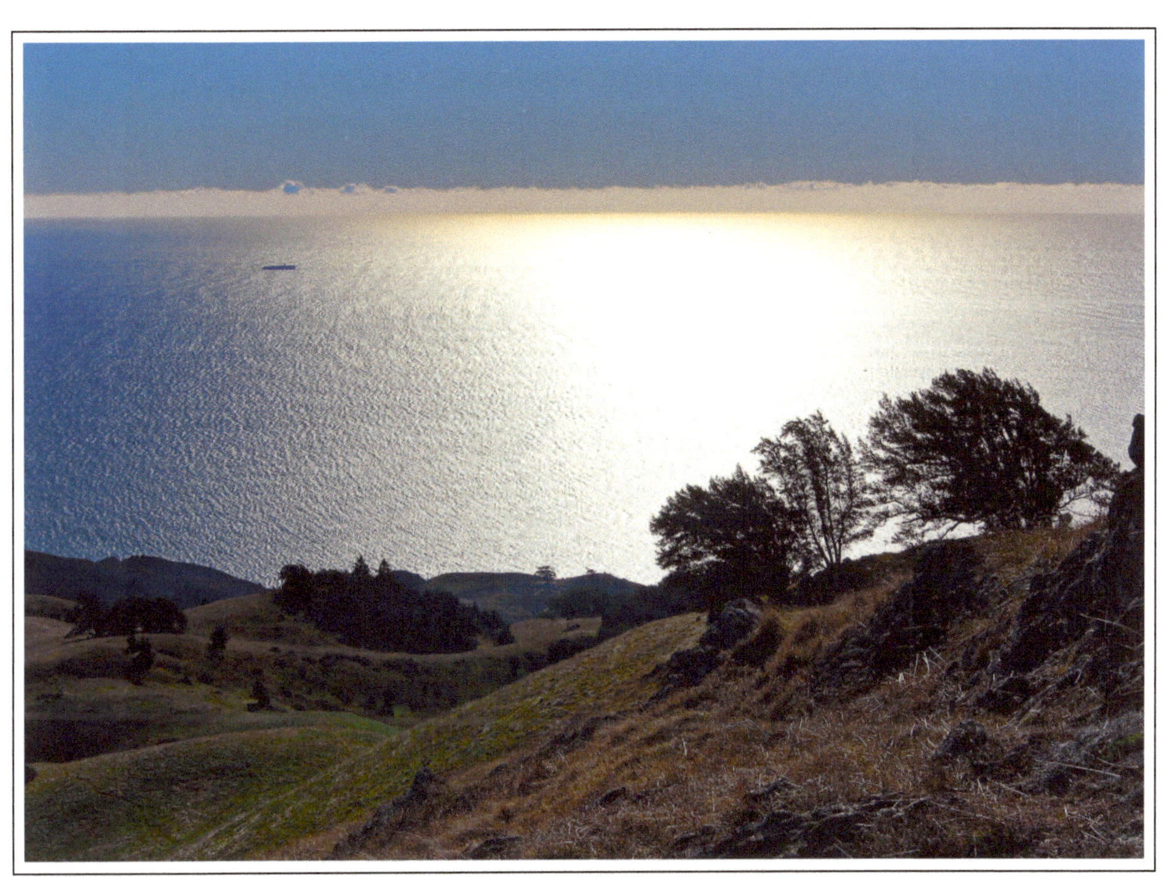

THE PLAIN OF SILENCE

The vastness of silence
in the stranger's embrace
reminds me of islands
beyond this empty place.

I take to the far road,
cross the plain of silence,
the unexplored abode
a star on the highland.

I have crisscrossed this plain,
arrived and crossed over
time and still time again
like a gypsy rover,

seeking beyond all words,
secrets beyond limits,
like multicolored birds
swathed in veils of spirits.

Never the arrival,
never the departure,
not even survival.
What beckons is rapture.

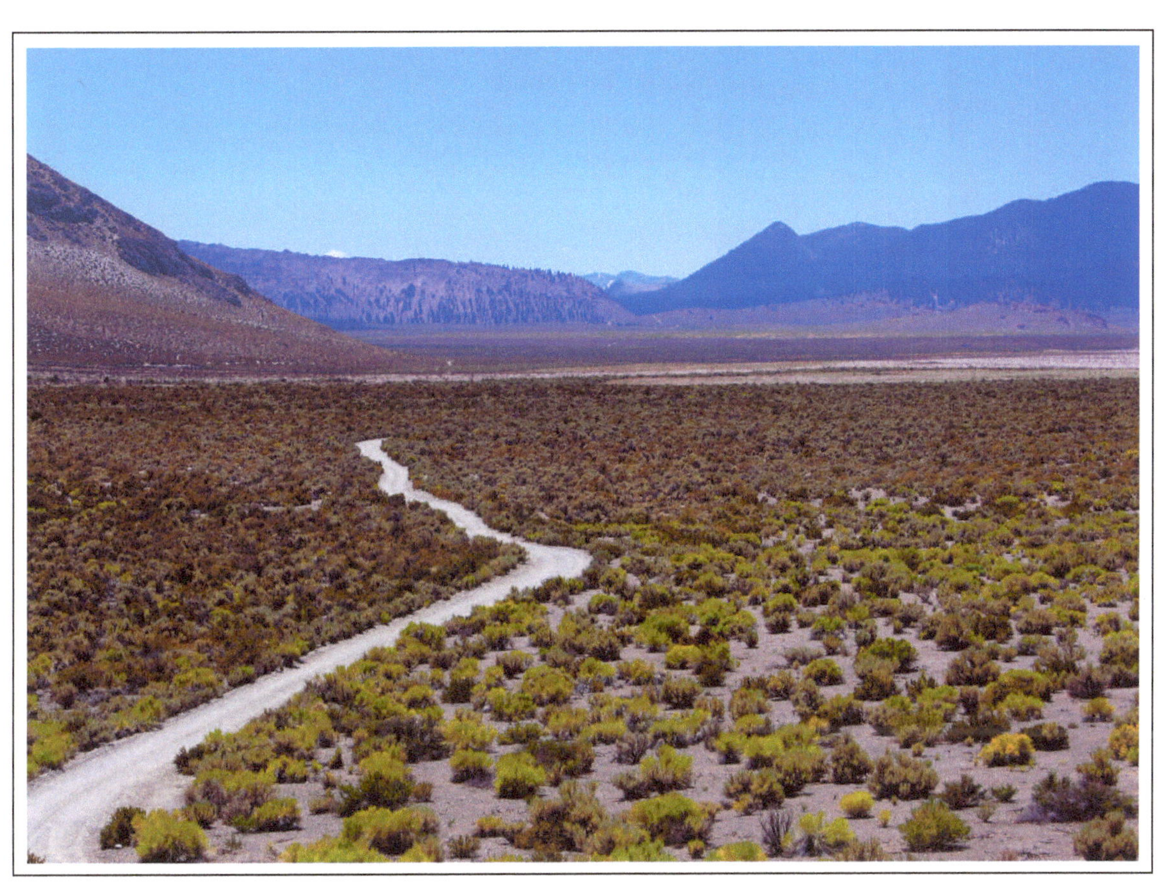

CANDLE TO THE SUN

I light my candle to the sun,
a small act of bold intent
calling forth the flaming orb
to rise resplendent on this day.

I hold my candle to the sun,
small flame striking a pose
to ward off hungry fires
until the battle's done this day.

Gone now my little flame,
though her scent still remains,
for blue-tipped with bravado
she rose to meet tomorrow's day.

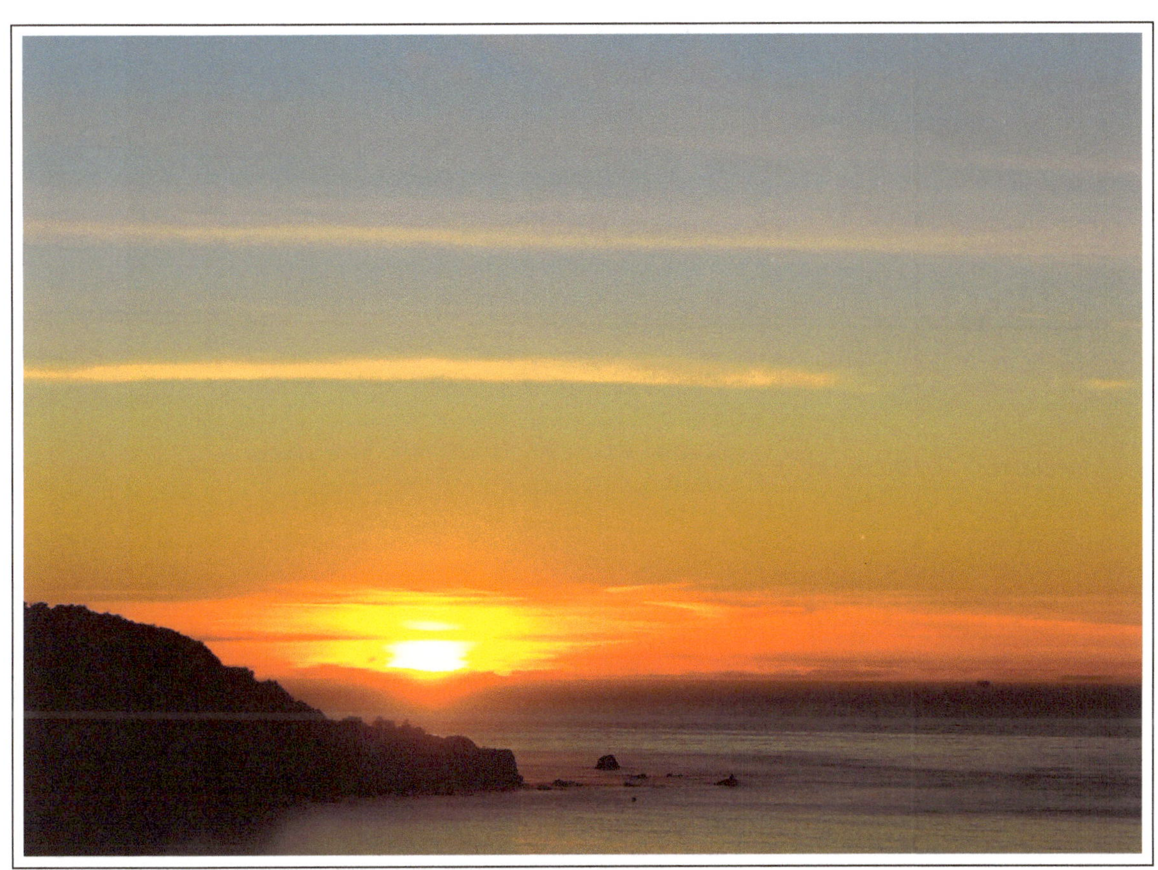

DAHLIA IN THE LIGHT

You caught my eye,
all ablaze
in the rays above.
Part of you all dazed,
a tear shedding
from deep within
where no one sees.

But I see and marvel
how one teardrop
can yet ignite
a thousand joys,
and each petal
a strand of light,
a candle to my night.

Burn me bright
in the fiery bliss
of your short life.
Raise me up
with each breath
of your blazing sigh,
my song of thee ignite.

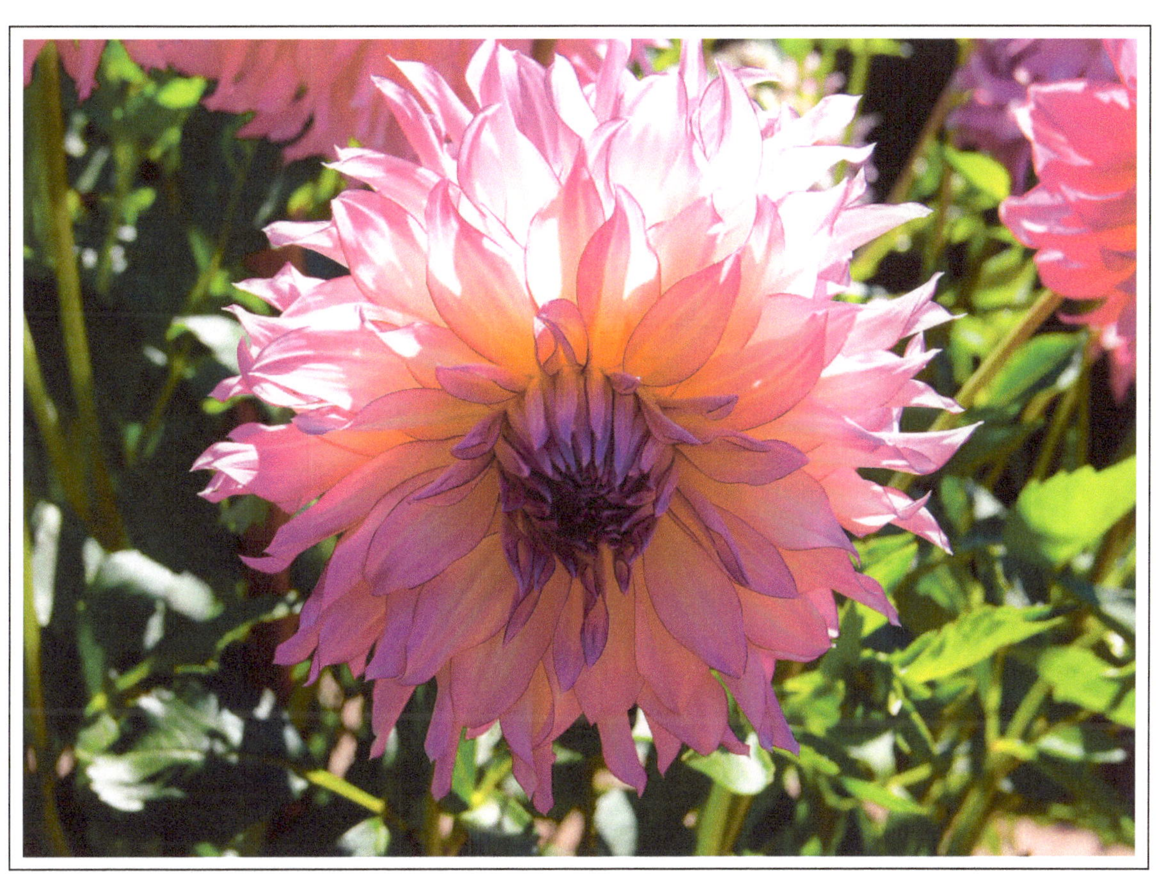

The New Vine

Swarms of red camellias fanning over the rail,
yellow pistils in clouds of purple-veined petals,
nuggets of pollen carried away by the gale.

All that sap like the blood cascading through my veins,
carried along streams of ancestors fanning forth
from that one familial font where all still remains.

The stream wells up along the hollows of my skin,
fans the air with ancestral seeds once I am gone,
only to be borne to the ocean once again.

Rooted to the ancestral font, I long for a line,
a wing of a prayer, to carry me away
to where fields await the planting of a new vine.

I will be the new vine, new histories entwine
to be scattered to the wind and surf once again,
feet dancing across the globe, free of all that's mine.

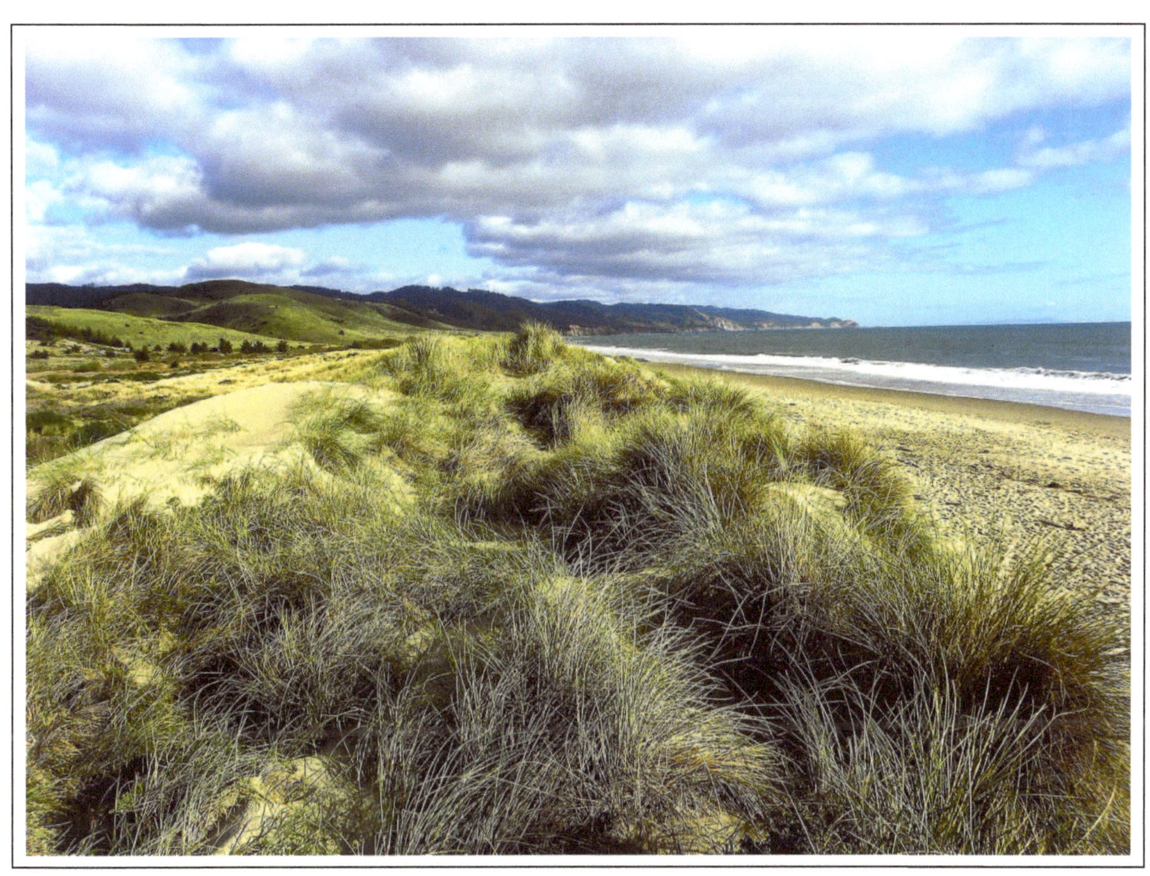

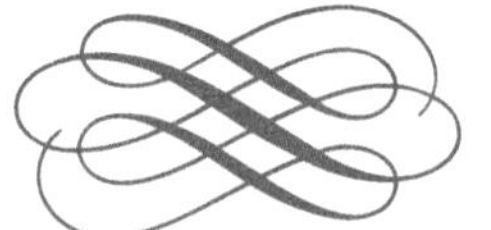

Part II
Leaning On Love

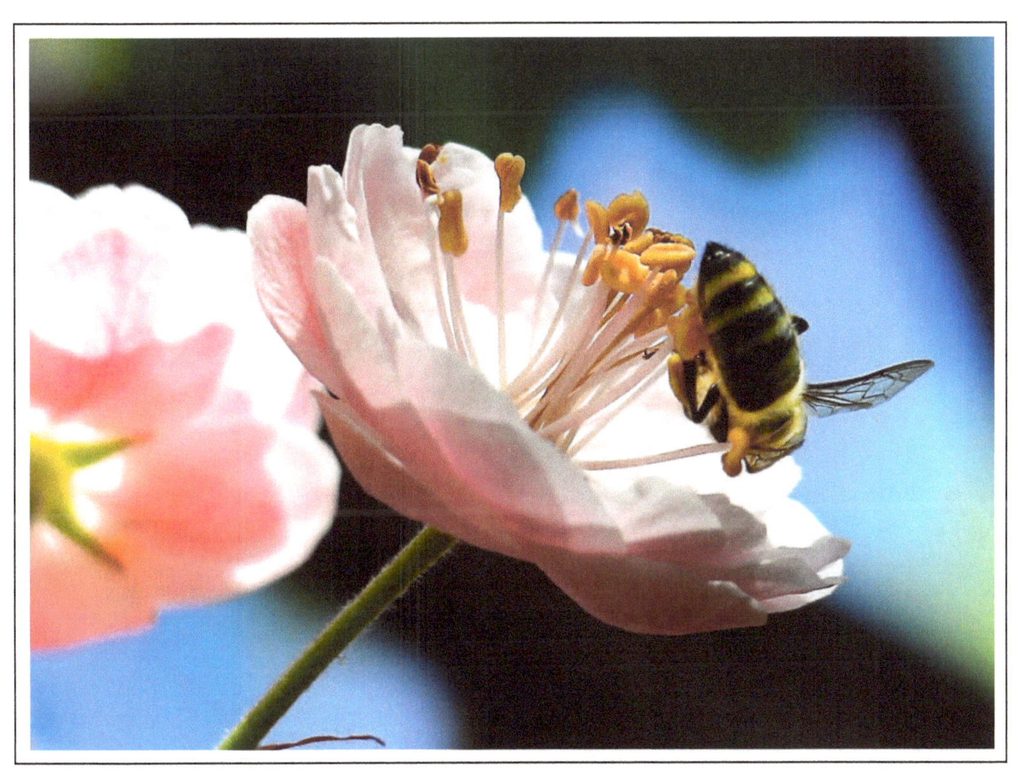

Grandma's Iron Stove

When I was a little girl, my grandmother tried to teach me to bake bread in an iron stove. It was a hopeless endeavor, my doll-sized loaves sitting on the kitchen table like petrified remnants from the Vesuvian eruption.

But my grandma's loaves, that was something else. To this day I remember the aroma, the taste and the texture of her freshly baked bread. Thick slices, dark grained, crisp on the outside, warm and moist on the inside, spread generously with home-whipped butter.

It takes a magician of nature's elements to bake bread in a wood-burning stove. Such was my grandmother. Only she could minister to its spitfire moods, giving us the daily bread that kept us going throughout the uncertain days of a farmer's life on the vast Pampa of the Argentine hinterland.

Daily she hovered over the burners, crouched with reverence before it's cavernous mouth. She stoked the fires and soon the aromas of stews, pies, and bread sallied forth through windows and doors calling in the field hands for lunch. Siesta time was indispensable for digestive recovery and resumption of labors.

Perched on the earthen floor of our small adobe hut, towering in a corner of the room that served as kitchen, dining room, and living room, radiating heat and nourishment from morn to dusk, the iron behemoth ruled the Olsen roost, and grandma was its high priestess.

I was but a little bird of a girl engulfed by the immensity of earth and sky, yet rooted to the center of the world by grandma's bread and the iron stove. To this day, no matter where my feet roam, home is where the bread is.

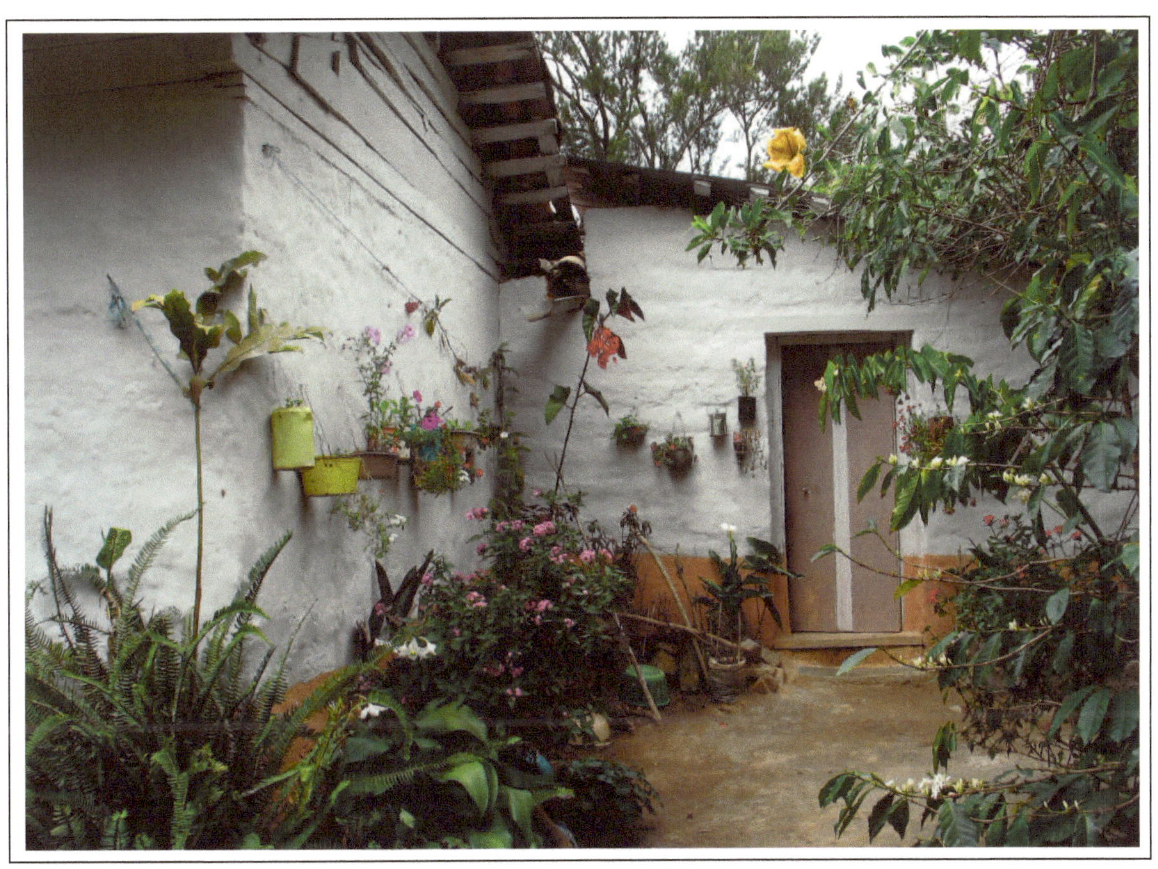

ANCESTRAL BOARS AND BOVINES

Back in the forest clearing of Herefordshire,
good ole' Thomas farmed and herded cattle.
There he stands crowning the genealogical tree,
in the year of our Lord fourteen fifty-three.

Further back in time (so says the Bard),
wild Hecanas roamed the mountains,
spearing boars, eluding Saxons,
abducting Viking lasses with tresses flaxen.

Edric of Pictkin flummoxed the conquering Norms.
They called these ragged bands the Silvan swarms,
for they slept nose to sky, come what may
– you know, to tighten up the soft spots for the fray.

Sounds familiar.
Such crazy notions sometimes fill my mind:

to herd cattle along the mountain face,
seek solace in a bovine gaze,
or hurl through the forest on the chase,
boar all ablaze, cow left behind in a daze.

Such are the churnings of rumpus ancestry
in the thumping blood of yours truly here,
in this year of our Lady Bard and Seer,
in this span of two-thousand and score more years.

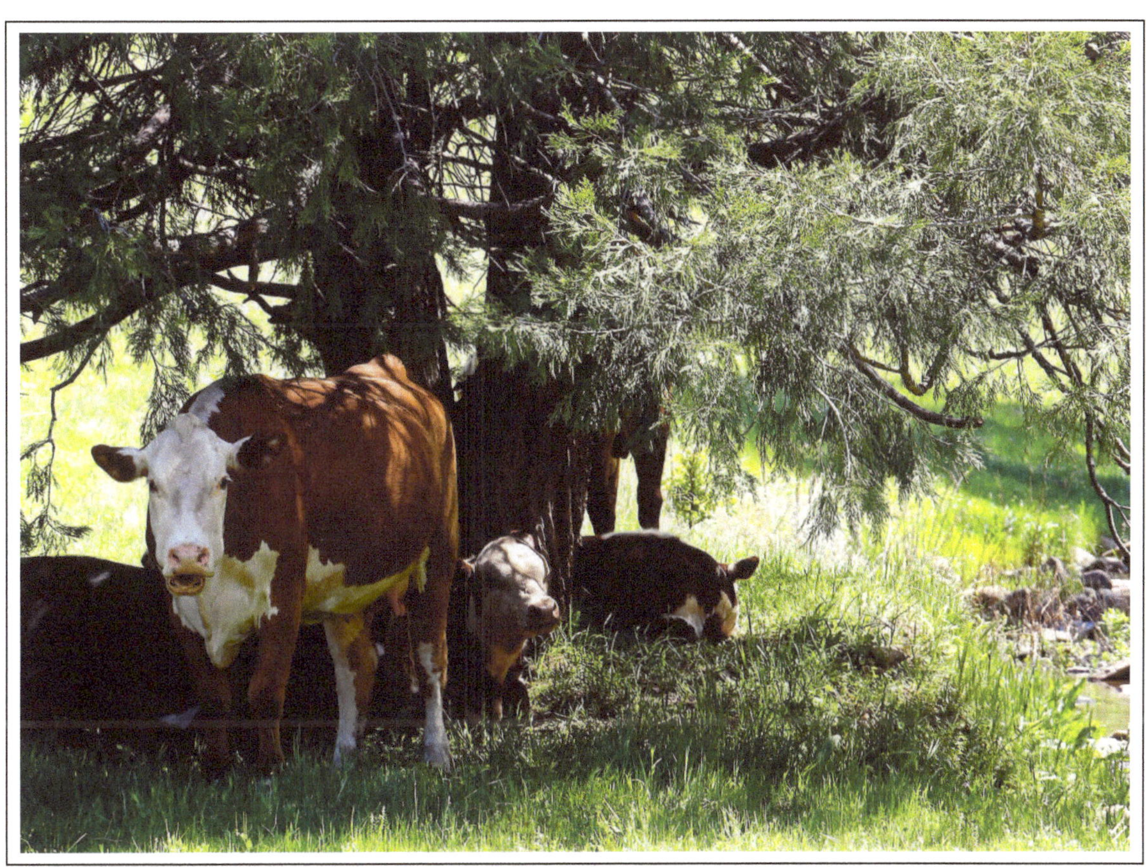

Coyote Friend

I hear you barking from fields beyond,
see you bounding up the slope ahead,
my pulse quickens to be with you again.
Wild and winsome in our youth
we ran the hills abreast,
yet I still surge forward on the quest.

You came to me a whimpering pup,
then made me laugh with your swagger.
You grew into a swift tracker,
spanning that liminal space
between the wild and the civilized.
Together we fled the lowland strife,
found respite on the oaken slopes.
When you bounded after deer,
inside my ribcage I beat the drum
until you were all done.

Together in that liminal divide
of the civilized and the wild
you taught me with your eyes
what no human ever taught
with the babble of their tongue:
that the chase alone
is reason for living,
not the catch but the joy
of keeping in sight
the quivering haunches in flight.

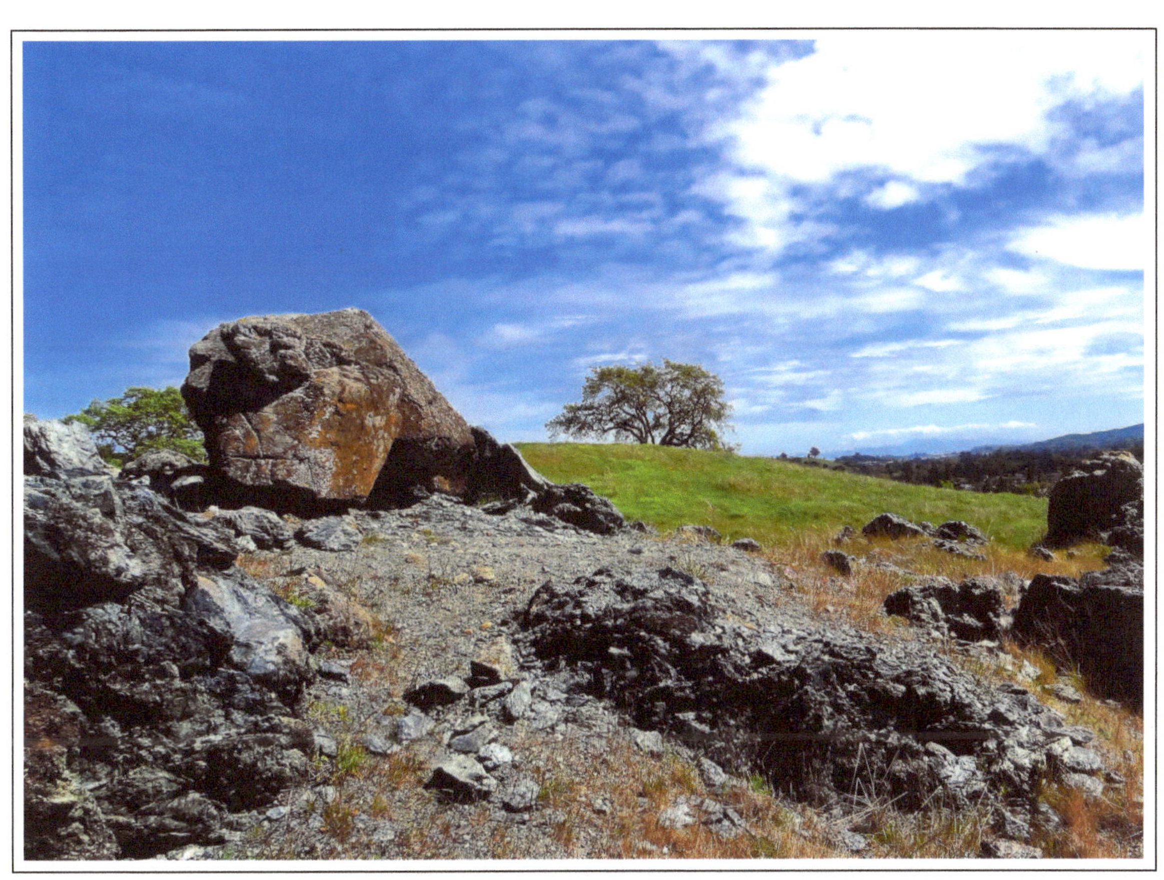

WHEN WINTER COMES

When winter comes,
felicity cloaks me in woolen garments,
and I marvel at the pearly light
of rain-drenched branches outside my window.

When winter comes,
I gaze at you through frosty glass,
then fling my coat over my shoulders,
and dash out to meet the cleansing chill.

When winter comes,
I follow the angling sun into wooded silence
where deer hoofs crackle on brittle twigs
and set my heart thumping.

When winter comes,
I count the hours of daylight,
while the moon's magnetic charm
pulls the blanket of night over my eyes.

When winter comes,
I recall the heat of the southern sun
like bread baking in an outdoor kiln,
like you lighting the fire that keeps me here.

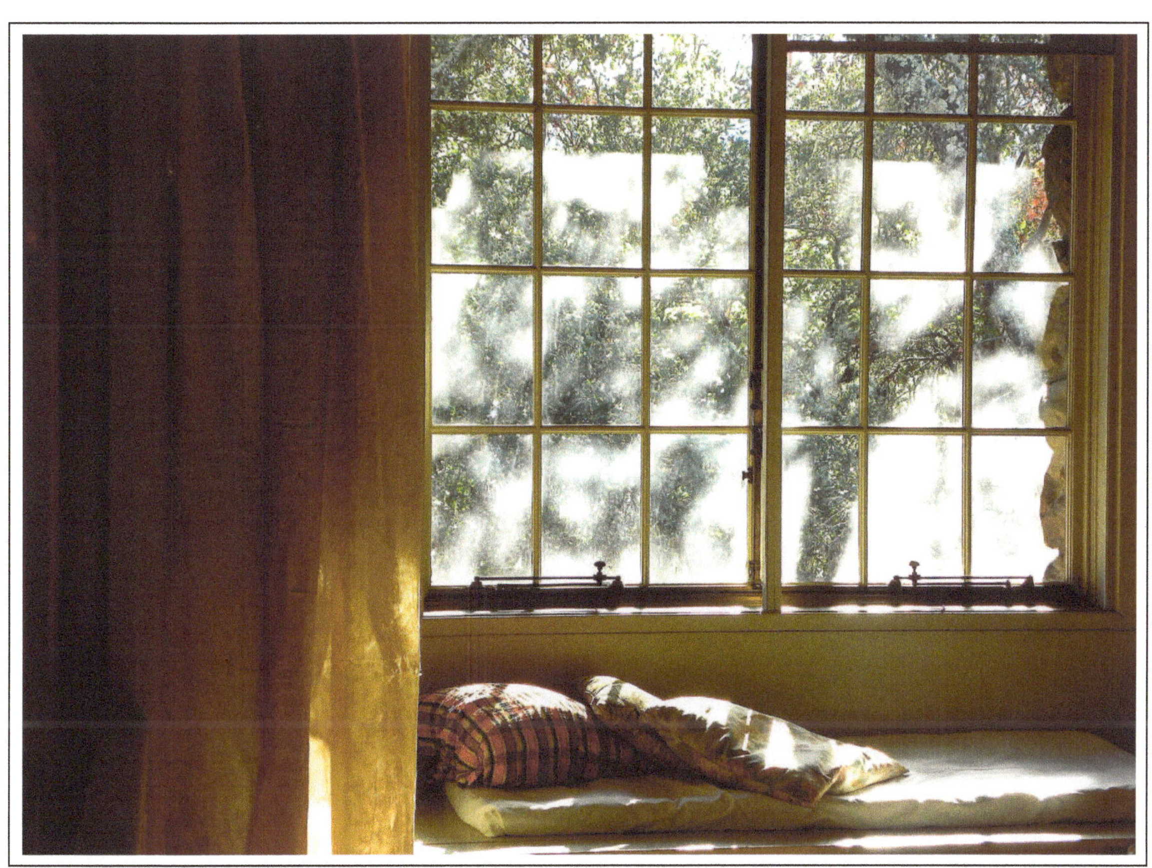

Tall Grasses In The Wind

See the tall grasses how they dance in the wind,
they dip and undulate as they waltz in the field.

When a sudden gale sends a whiplash across the pond,
they do not resist the charge but bend with grace.

When adversity comes rolling down the mountainside
I will dance like the tall grasses in the glen.

When the gale stops I will walk on with poise,
bending and dipping on the trail of the sweeping tides.

I cannot resist the onslaughts that come with living,
but I can waltz along the way like the grasses on the hill.

With each bend I am made resilient for forgiveness;
with each bend I am made worthy of love.

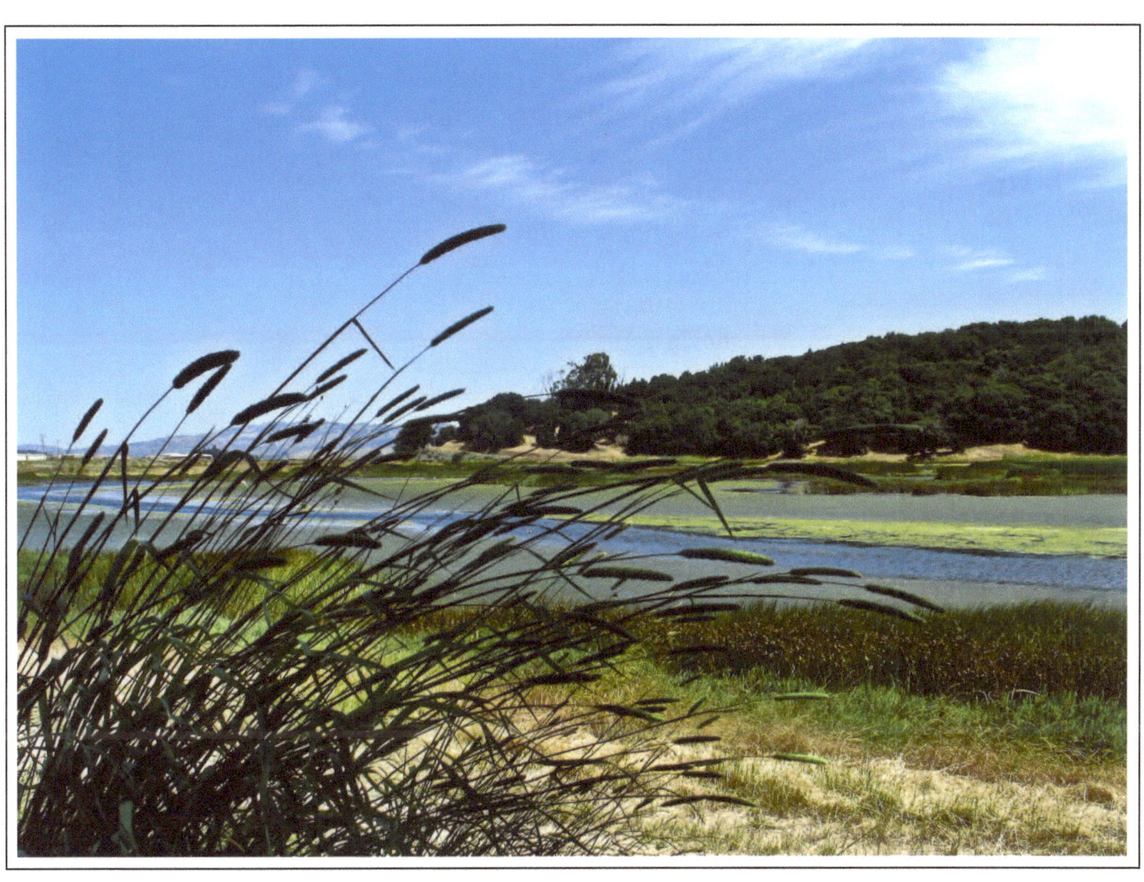

MAYBE YOU

Cow at the gate,
pig in the pot,
horse in the stall,
man who rakes hay.
What more could I want
in the span of this day?
Maybe you,
hovering nearby,
fickle and spry,
here till I die.

You on the sideline,
in the half-light,
disappearing in dark light,
reappearing in limelight.
You, out there and in here,
hoofing like a deer,
you, flushing me whole
with bellows in my soul.
Breath of life stay
until I pass away.

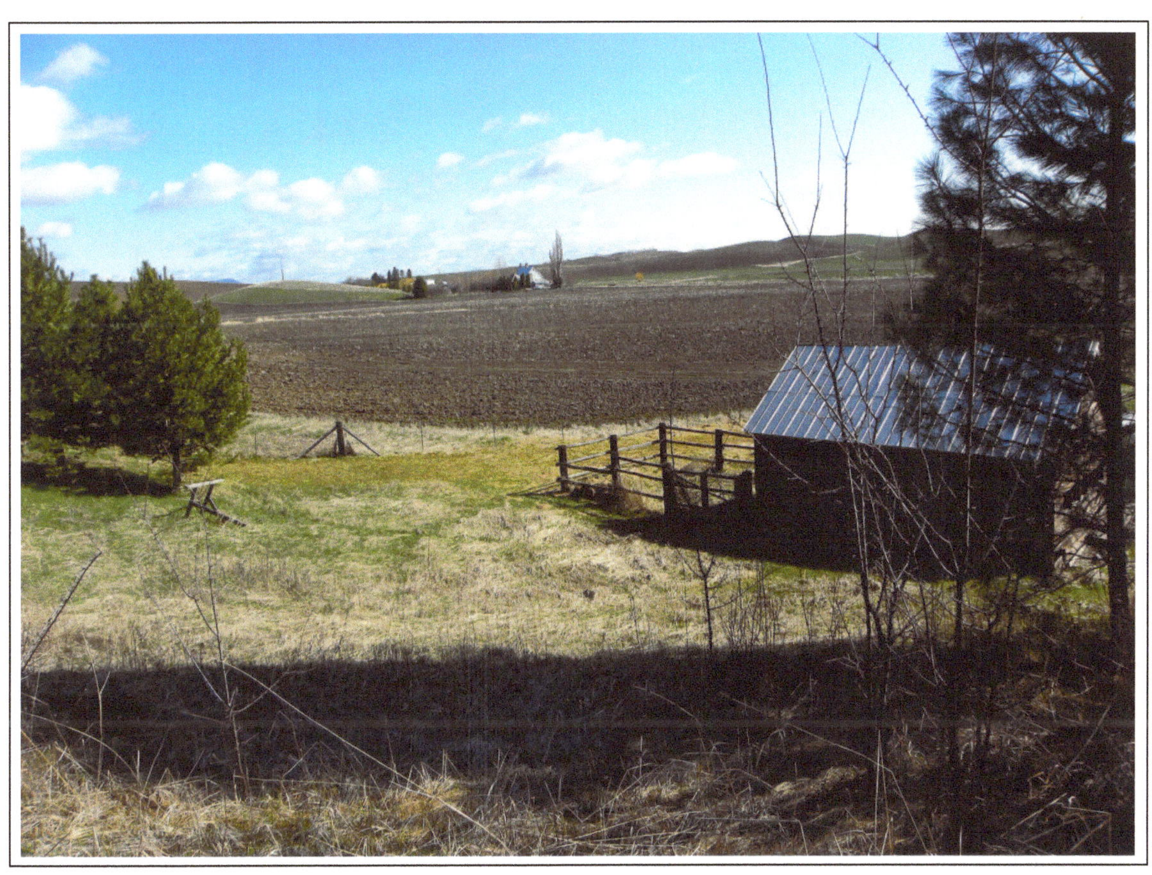

THE LINE

With eyes glued to the line
that separates earth
from the boundless blue,
I soar like the eagle,
and have no fear,
anchored as I am right here
where the human heart
and alien spirit meet.

Alien spirit, denizen of the blue,
You are what I will become
when the line breaks and I tumble
into the vast panorama
of the ever-unfolding story.

But for now, a tablecloth
on the mountain top
invites me to tea and scones.
You are there too, my love,
and I am happy for the line
that still reigns me in
as I stand on the precipice
of all that is yet to come.

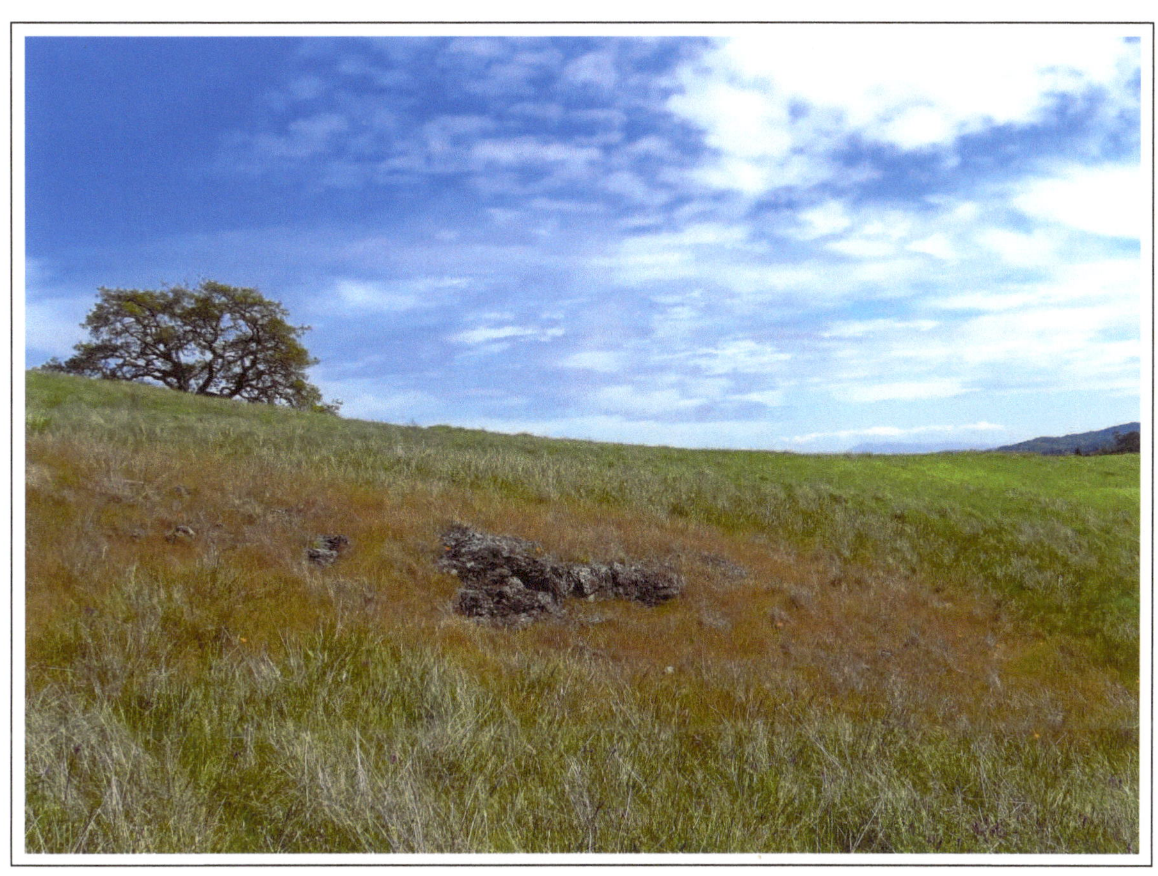

ON DYING IN LOVE

I thought of you
on coming home.
(You were already there.
Having spanned a thousand nights,
dying was your art.)

I took the plunge
without my wings.
(You were already there.
Having sipped a thousand teas,
patience was your name.)

I stepped inside
and looked within.
(You were already there.
Having seen the world a flame,
love was all you had.)

I softly asked
"do wings grow back?"
You whispered in my ear,
"Wings are where your heart burns
and there I am with you, dear."

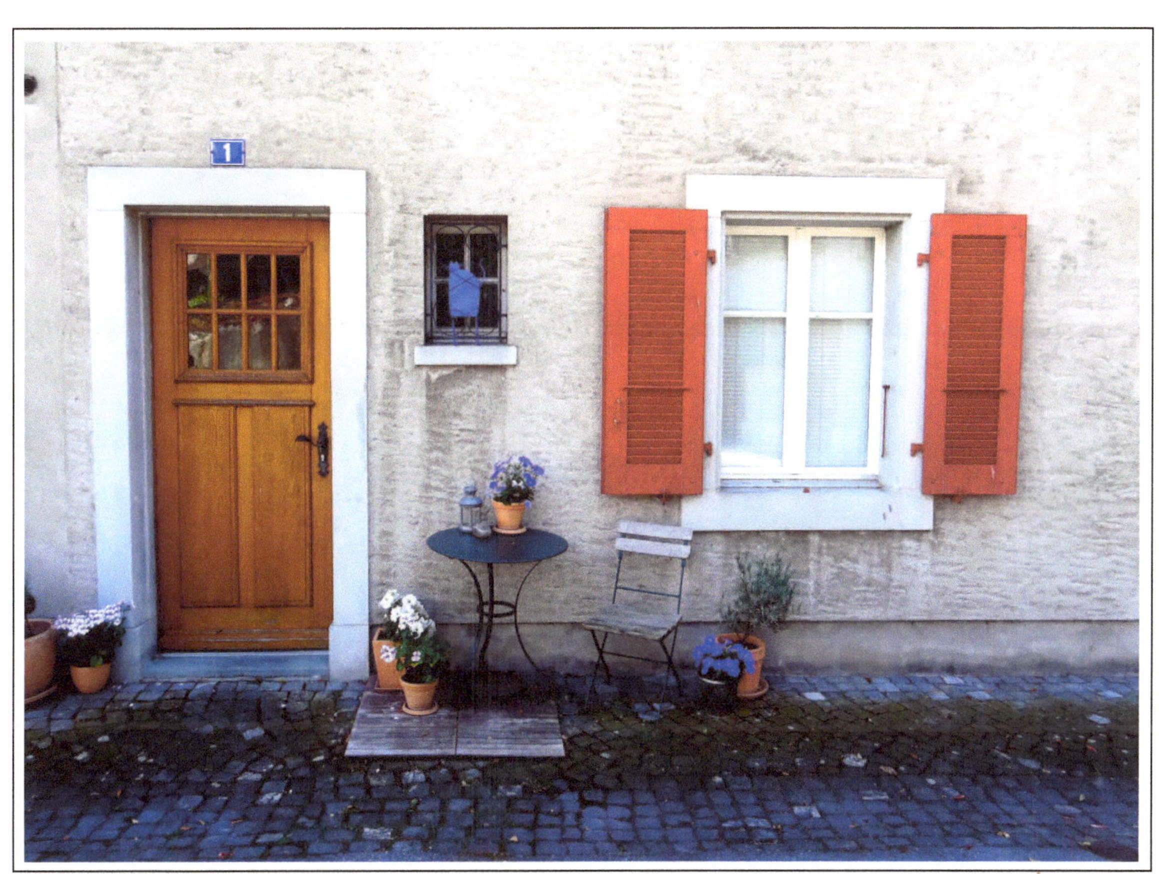

DESIRE

Desire hidden in flowing words
atop lofty peaks at heaven's port.
Then a soft ripple of thirst,
fingers reaching across the ice.

A sudden fluvial surge
plunging us down the abyss.
Fury of love in pursuit
sprinting along the banks.

Passions spent in the plunge,
an ever-widening amble
carries us to a vast embrace
in the depth of oceanic bliss.

Wrapped in the solace of time,
when we hobble along hand in hand,
desire will still simmer in our bones,
fire pressed between our palms.

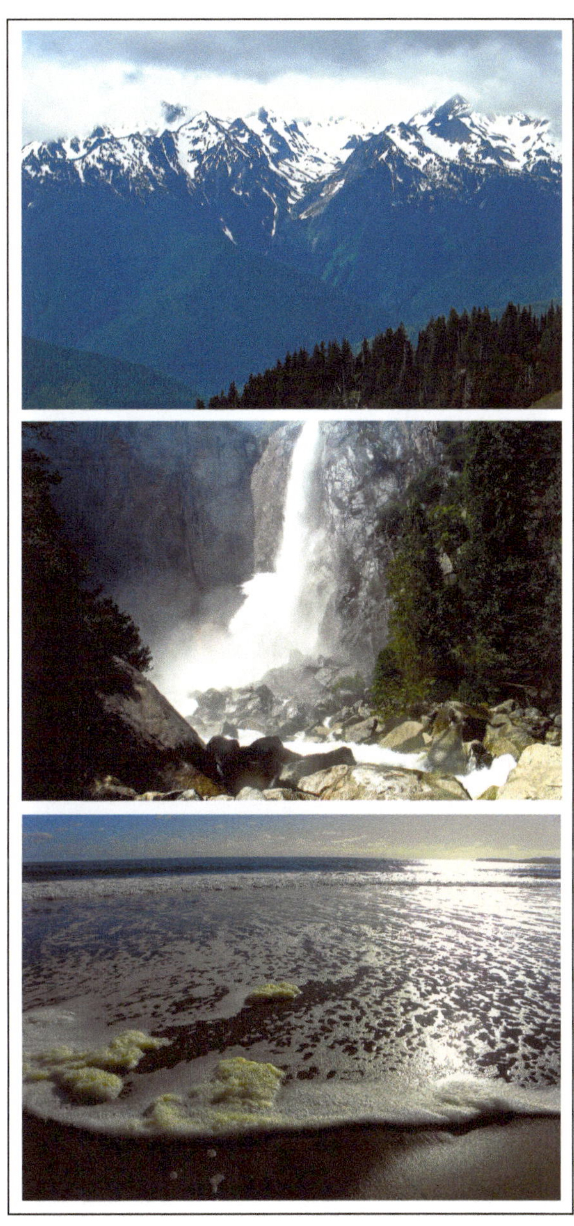

Canticle
(To A Rose In Bloom After The Rains)

Meandering on that hidden path,
I saw you standing there,
all the people plucking at your sleeves,
guzzling every exhalation of your breath,
your face a flaunting blush.
I saw you standing there,
and knew you had come back to me,
even as you passed me by,
your face awash in dew.

I turned to follow
and sought you in your bower,
stole a kiss under a Spring shower
in that place where none dared look.

Now, only a whiff of you remains
in my sealed book of canticles.
And yet, I long to see
the loveliness of you
permeating the whole wide world.
I think, yes I think
I may unseal the book,
take you from the pages,
and scatter you abroad.

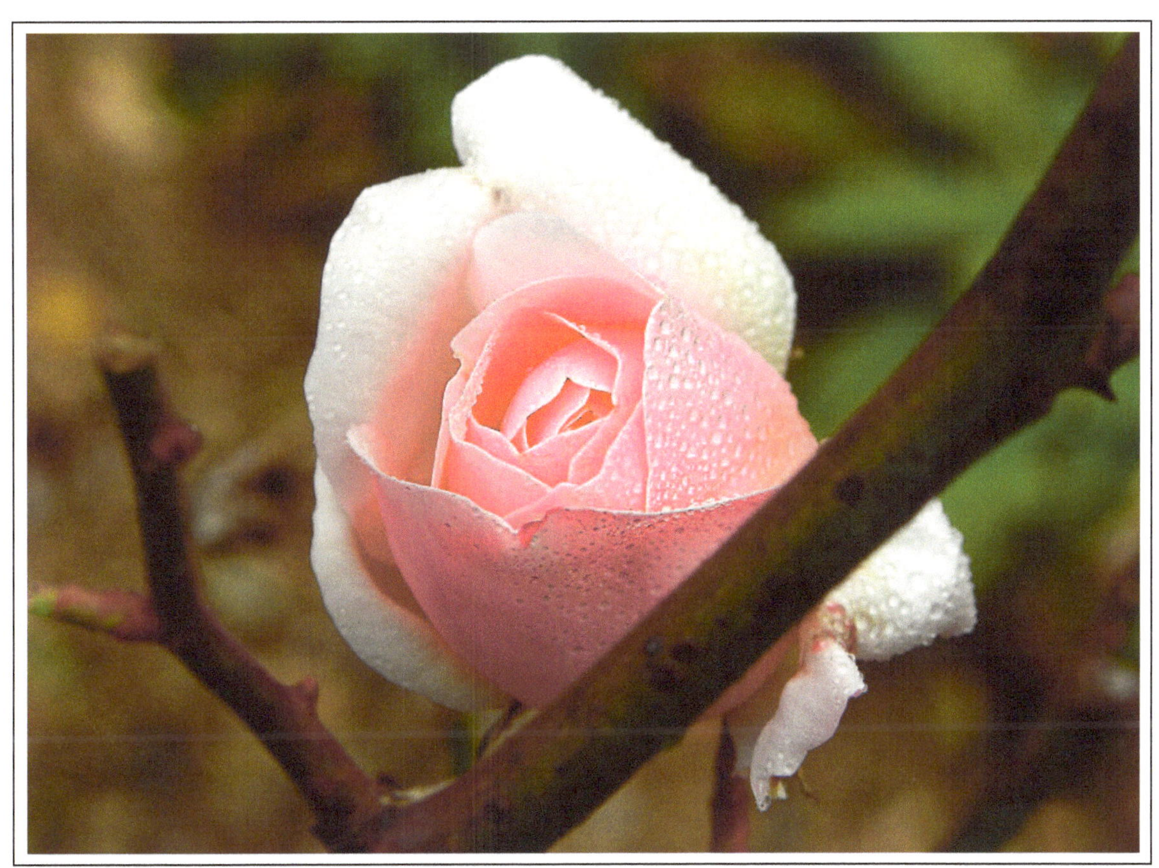

On Seeing Love

Today I rose in dawning mist,
trees unfurling in a veiled kiss.

Eyes to ground up the steep incline,
nothing did I see that rose sublime.

When suddenly in full presence
loomed the tallest luminescence,

calling me back to a far land
where pines towered above the sand.

Many a times I walked this way
in the glare of a sunlit day,

but love grows dim beneath the sun,
while dawn unveils a finer spun

of tents that billow in the breeze,
sheltering lovers from the heat.

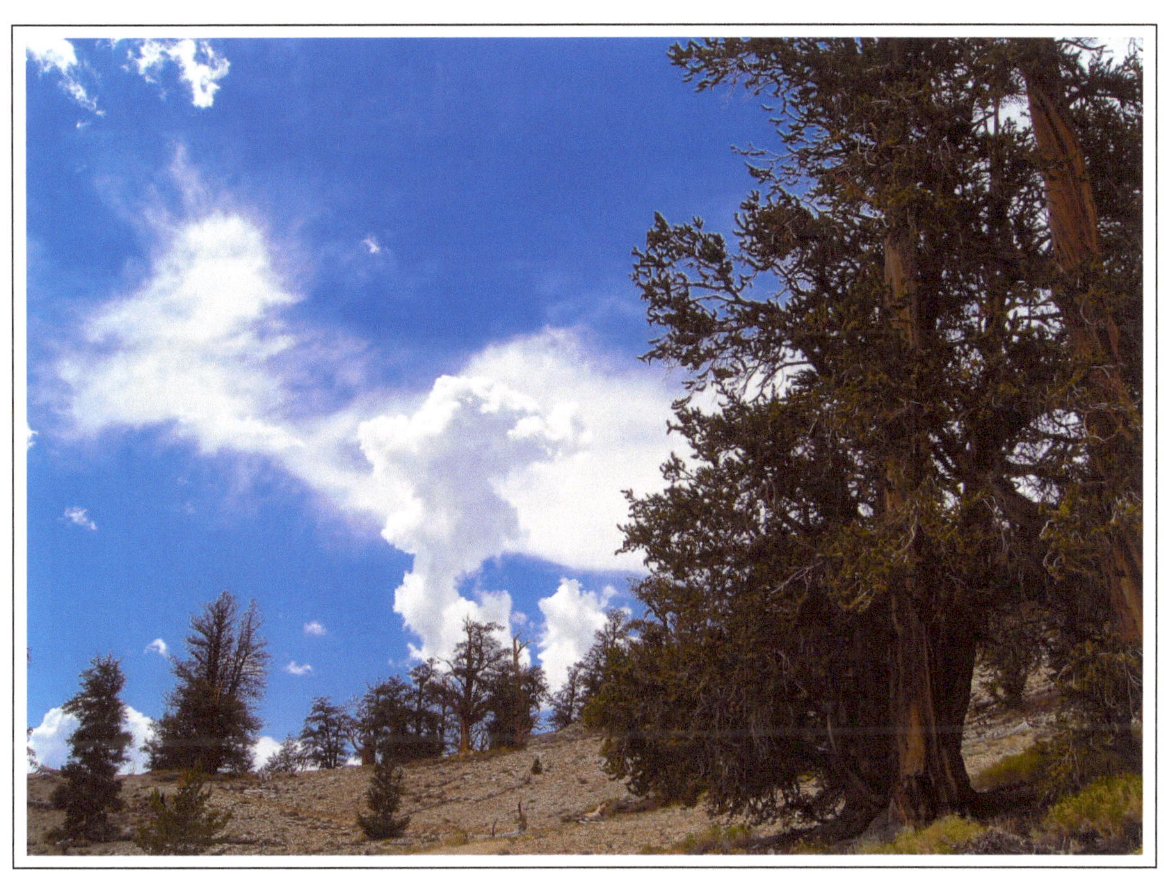

REFUGE

I take refuge in silence
from the clamor
of a world gone mad
where strange beings
pursued by furies
build fences
shovel cement
burn rubber
whirl in smog
dance macabre
to electric saws
marking time

I take refuge in silence
where the only sound
is of butterfly wings
falling feathers
sprouting seeds
ripening vines
magic berries
in liquid flight
quickening joy
a fluttering murmur
whispering in my ear
"I love you"

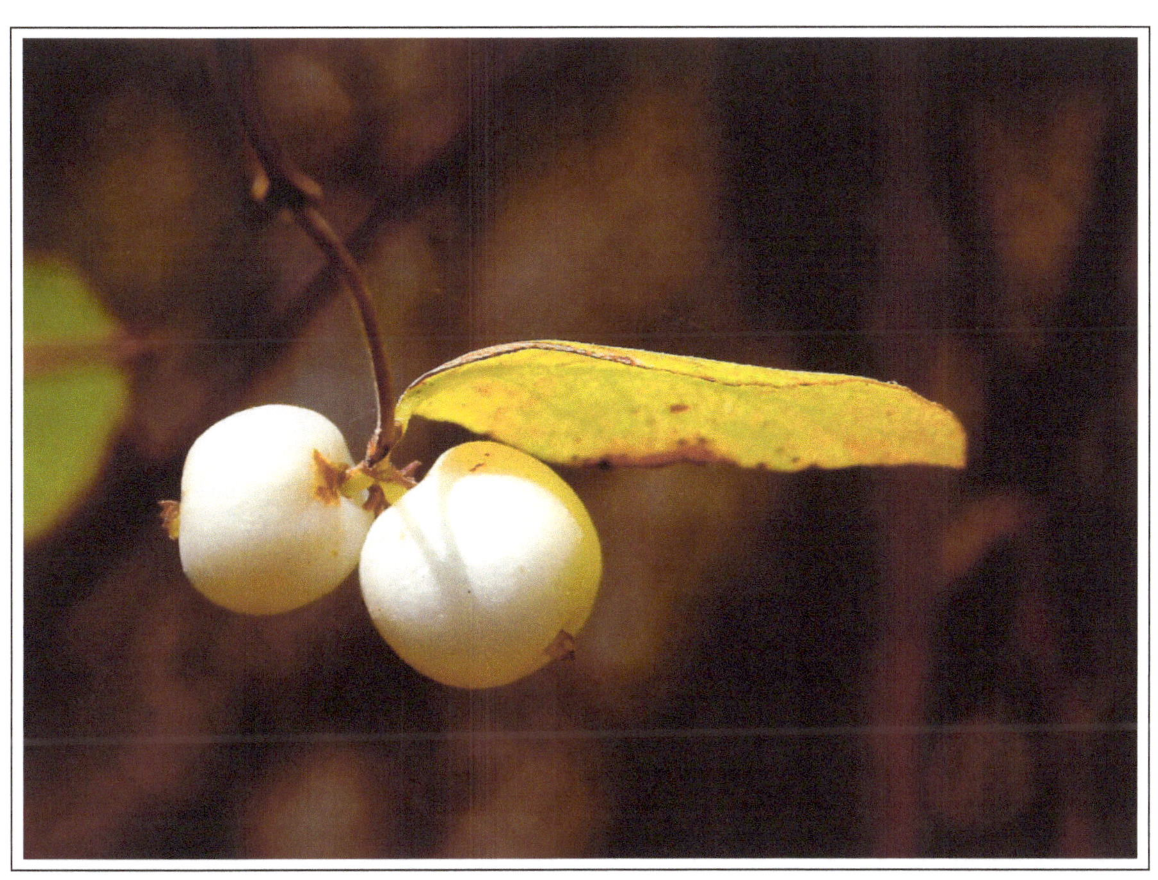

ON SEEING THE INVISIBLE
(For Haiku Dave)

Standing above the fog he surveys the unseen, memories rising up from times past, faint drumbeats bearing messages from uncounted and discounted ancestors.

Apache, Tolteca, Maya, Moro — all dancing in his blood, sounding the drumbeat ever louder up through the fog, up through the soles of his feet.

He wears white to honor the day of the Sun, the day when all stands still, infusing a drop of white to stem the darkening of the sky before all memory is gone.

But he remembers. He readies for the hunt, he crouches, his eyes sharp as the eagle's. He sees what no one else sees, an image from a fog-robed world filling his lens.

Hand steady at the base, finger poised to release the shutter, the drums cease, the world stops spinning, silence and suspension are one.

I look across the horizon hoping to catch a glimpse of his prey, but already the whirr of the shutter signals capture.

He turns triumphant and says, "Look, I got it!" I look to see what I could not see before — looking back at me my hidden self revealed.

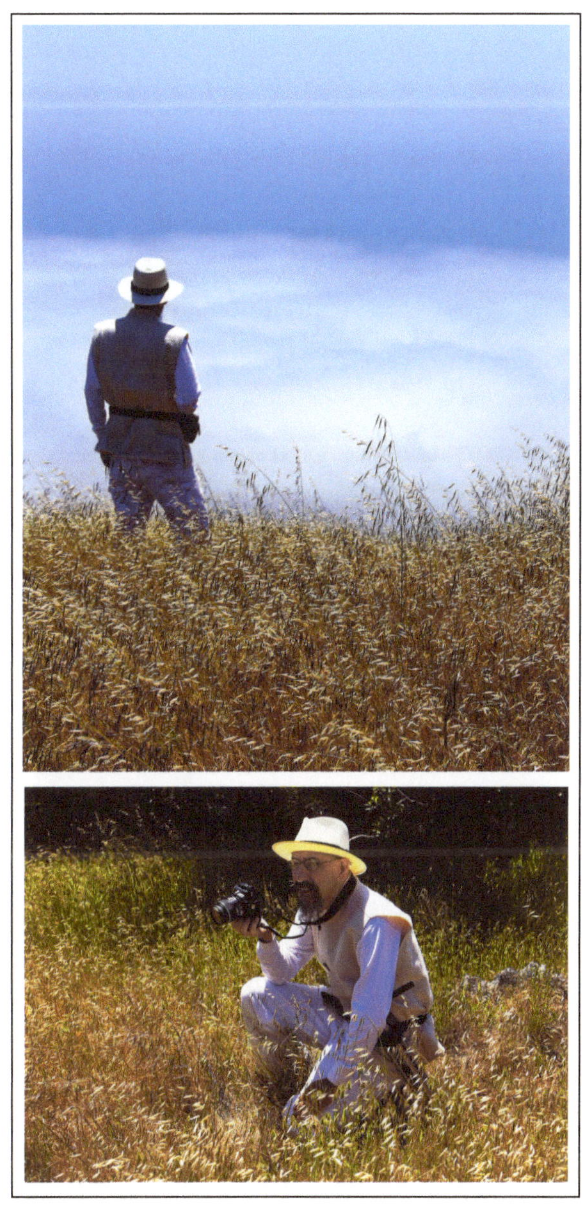

White Petal Flame

See the white flowers,
such springtime simplicity,
innocence and felicity,

laughing and bubbling forth
from dark winter depths
in full unadorned strength.

Even after heartache,
tears like snowflakes,
I will rise like white flowers,

reach up with great power,
grab hold of a white star,
and burn the night sky

with white streaks of fire
until all that remains
is a white petal flame.

And then
    I will
        love again.

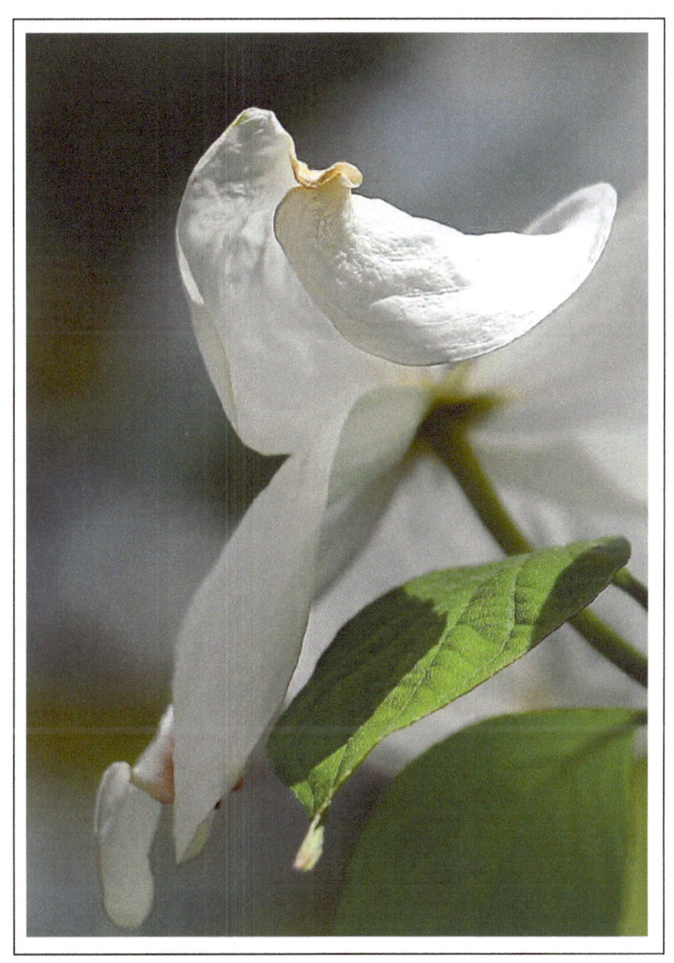

Beryl's Sofa

When I was a child living in Buenos Aires, I eagerly anticipated those sultry summer afternoons in my godmother's flat, curled up in her sofa chair with book in hand. Staples of English literature: Dickens and Thackeray, Austen and Gaskell, Carroll and Collins, Tennyson and Wordsworth, the Bronte sisters, and the terrors of Shakespeare and the King James Bible. And though much of what I read was incomprehensible to my unseasoned mind, that sofa promised me the world.

I read because it felt important, because the letters and words felt like clues etched on broken bits of antique shards strewn along the pathway of a dense forest. One day I would find my way out of the forest and the mystery of the world would be revealed right there where the land dips into the open arms of the sky.

So I read, on and on through the setting of the day. Behind me, the French windows opened onto a small balcony, beckoning the hot air to billow through the gauze of white curtains, ghostly forms undulating and gently caressing my bare arms. Sluggish sounds of voices, cars and buses wafted up the seven floors, then paused at the open windows, wispy updrafts hovering like harried vampires begging entry into the hallowed tower. But I never looked behind. To my child's mind seven floors up was where my godmother held court, a guardian angel of the lofty realm of books and learning.

Beryl was her name, like the ringing of a bell, like the brilliance of the blue-green crystalline mineral, like the clairvoyance of a soul-hunter.

I visited Beryl a few years ago. Same flat, same sofa positioned with its back to the French windows. The vampires are now gone and Beryl has ceased hunting souls, yet the books are still there to peruse in the lull of the hot summer afternoon as Beryl rests her weary bones at siesta time.

I take my place in the old sofa, a much tighter fit than when my scraggly bird-legs folded beneath me. I pick up Wordsworth once again. The afternoon hums on. I close my eyes. Somewhere in the back of my mind I hear a soft bell ringing. It is Beryl shuffling in with tea and scones to awaken me from my slumber, words of Wordsworth left adrift on the forest floor. It was another time, another place.

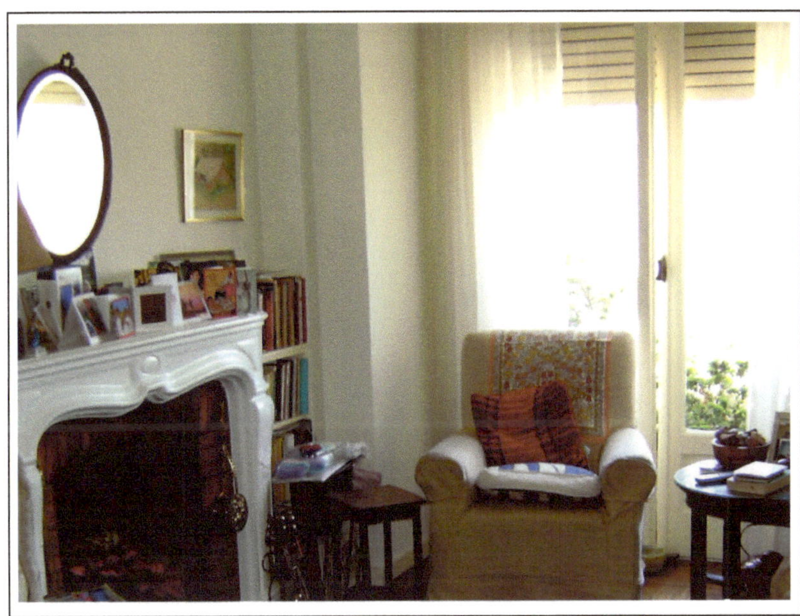

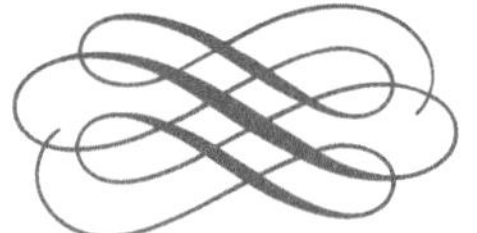

Part III
Kissing The Sky

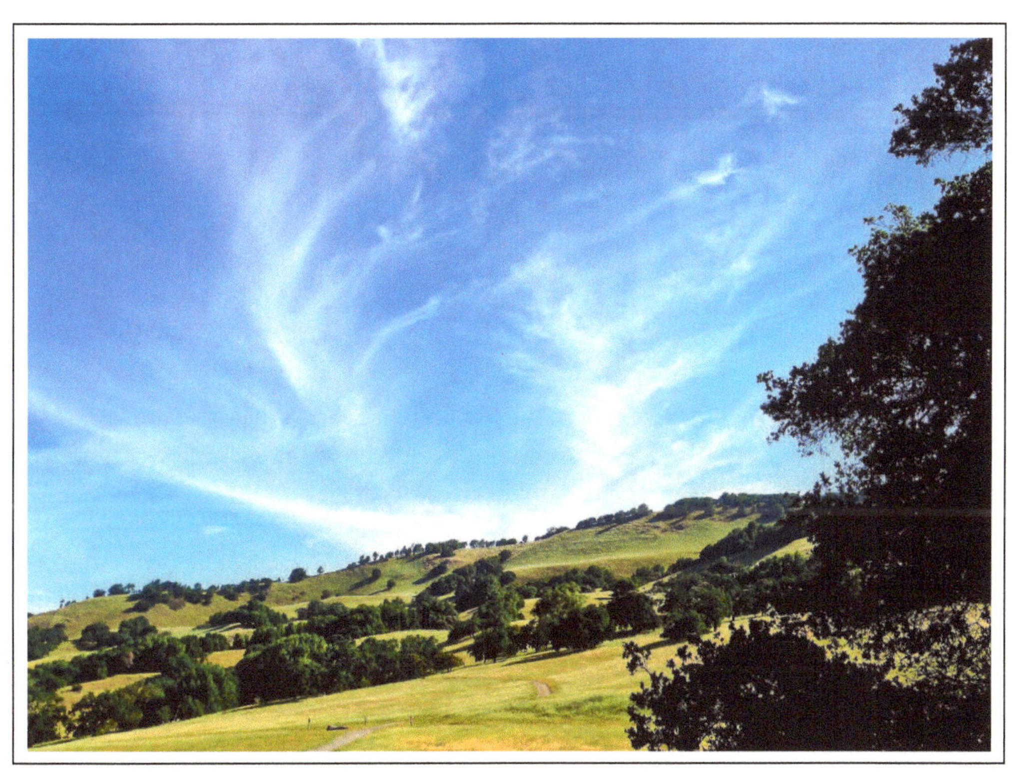

THERE IS SOMETHING ABOUT MY DECK

At the break of dawn I step out to greet the rising sun glimmering through the trees, rays dancing with the leaves, birds already busy with the chatter of their morning congress.

Two black crows squawk at each other, pitch rising and falling. They do this every morning. No rhyme or reason, yet it all makes sense.

Bees and butterflies come. The hummingbird hovers before me in greeting, then beelines for the flowers to drink nectar emitted in the secret of the night.

Which reminds me, there is something about my deck in the secret of the night…

Skunks and rabbits come; field rats too. All creatures great and small come for succulent leaves and flowers – even though I now keep the bitters at ground level and sweetmeats hanging high from the beams of the upper deck. I have won the battle, but they still come, haunted by the memory of feasting on my guileless offerings.

A young doe, making her rounds at dusk, jumps the fence at midnight, alighting on soft-padded hooves. Thinks I don't see her from behind my bedroom curtains. Standing still, she gazes out to the grove below, waiting for her Romeo.

Cats come too, each claiming space to answer an inner call. The grey one perches on the railing, keeping watch for denizens of the dark. The black one, who runs from me in the day, sleeps on my deckchair at night. The young ginger sits hypnotized before my potted lavender. Every morning I check out the pot to see what I've missed. I am still bemused.

There is something about my deck that surprises. With the winged, the hoofed and the pawed, I too feel stretched here in this liminal space of containment and sanctuary tucked away at the edge of wilderness.

Here we are called to be beyond what nature has intended. Birds legislate, crows sound sensible, hummingbirds hum salutations, cats decipher mysteries, and deer enact the eternal love scene on the balcony.

And I? I surf on sunbeams through the ridges of my mind, sail on moonbeams to the heart of secret gardens, balloon from one star to another.

There is something about my deck…something.

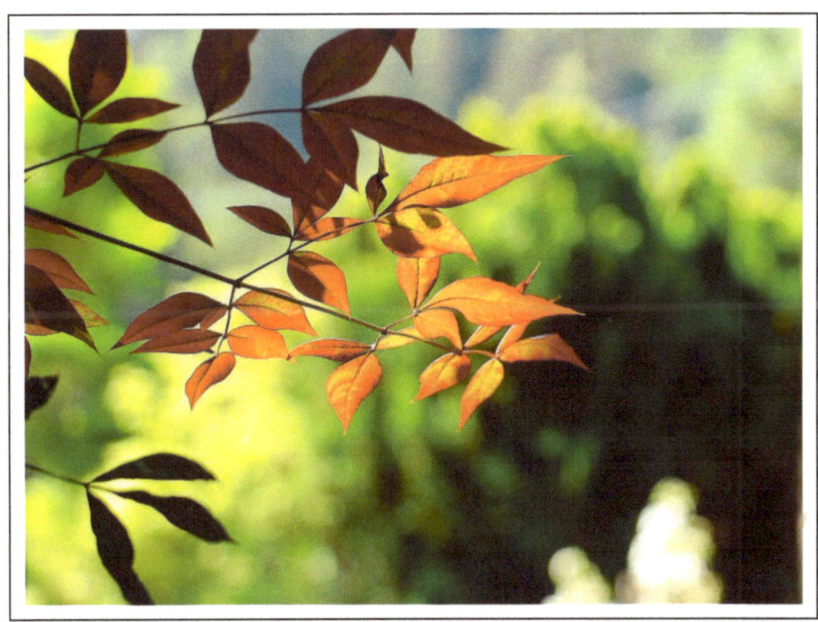

Nothing Will Ever Be The Same

Into the garden
cup of morning tea
sunshine filtering
through Fall gold
passing
from blush to ash

All around
a congress of birds
in thrilling abandon
yet here I stand
sheltered
invisible

Then something shifts
a gust through the trees
veils whisked off
to uncover
astonishing
nakedness

Sparrow flits to the fence
sunders heaven with tones
that send me reeling
above rooftops
above skyline
into the blue

Timeless yet time passes
falling to solid earth
now seeing
all made new
in the span
of ecstasy

Dissolved to blue
yet the day beckons
to make shadows real
still
    nothing
        will ever
            be the same

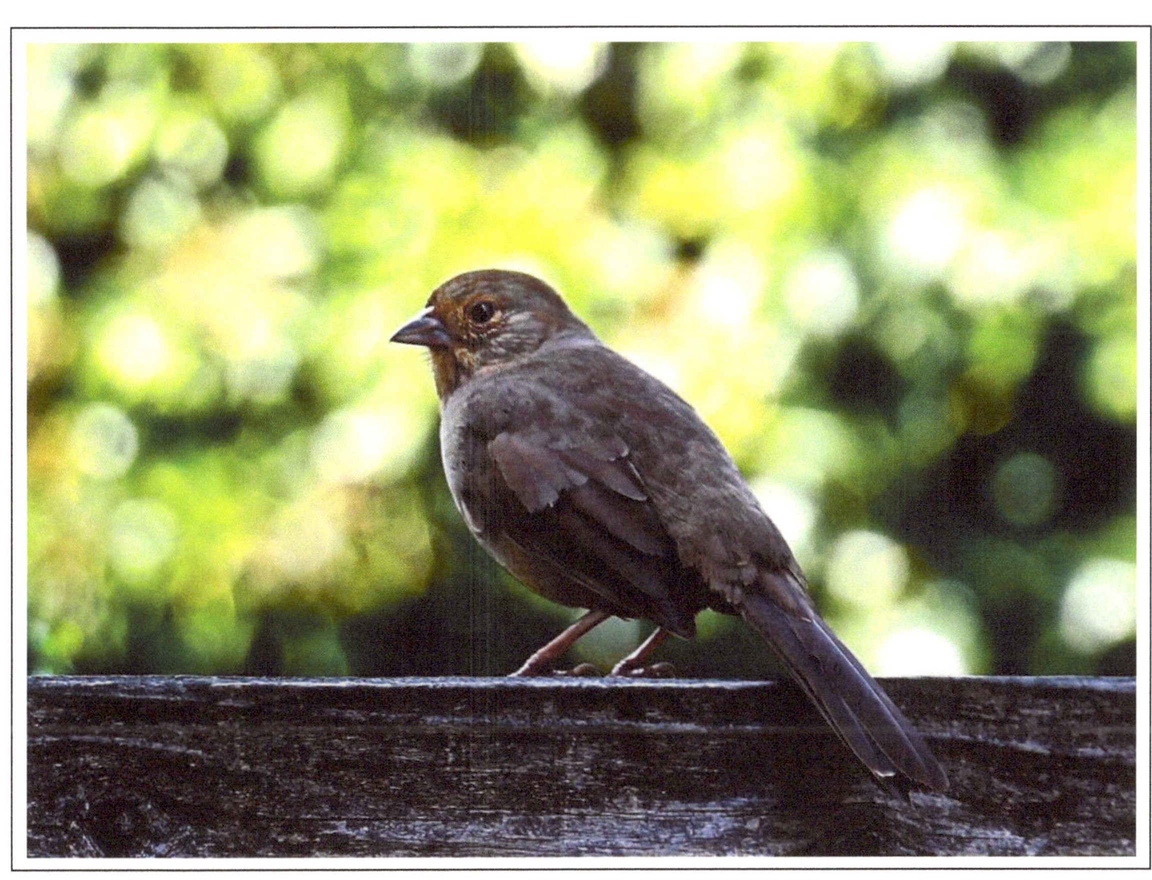

OUT OF THE NOW

Upon waking, silence greets me with the echoing timbre of a vanishing moon. Through my open window, the sky lies heavy with the purple promise of a blazing sunrise.

Yet all stands still, suspended, waiting for the cosmic clock to strike the campanile of a new dawn, to light the fires for the new day.

I strain to rise from the bedrock of dreams, but a strange weight impedes all motion, holding me down inside an eternal Now.

So this is it? Just this? All past and future gone? Let me out, Lord Shiva of the dancing flames! Let me out, Lord Krishna of cowbells and anklets!

With a crash of cymbals I snap back into the bliss of motion.
Back to the moon's gossamer tilt as she closes the book of dreams.
Back to the purple garment of the sun's ascension as he opens the book of days.
Back to the whirling center of cosmic mind that dances upon the rock of all times.

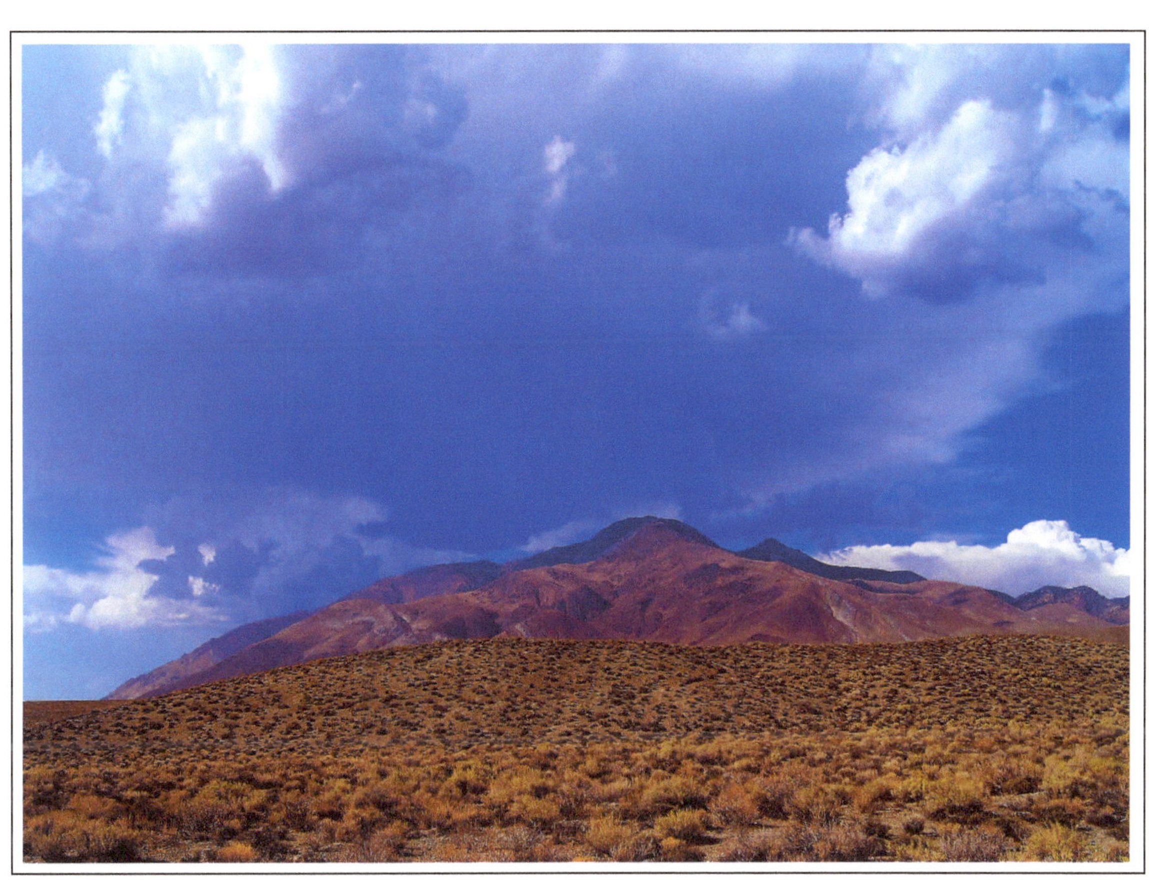

The Road Of Longing

Around the bend a far horizon,
sun melting clouds far-flung.
On my tongue a song unfurled
calling forth future worlds.

This moment but a fragment
of a longing more magnificent,
with vivid colors from the past
fleshing out the daily forecast.

Lean firm into the open road
for today is but one episode,
one sign of what's to come,
all the longing in every atom.

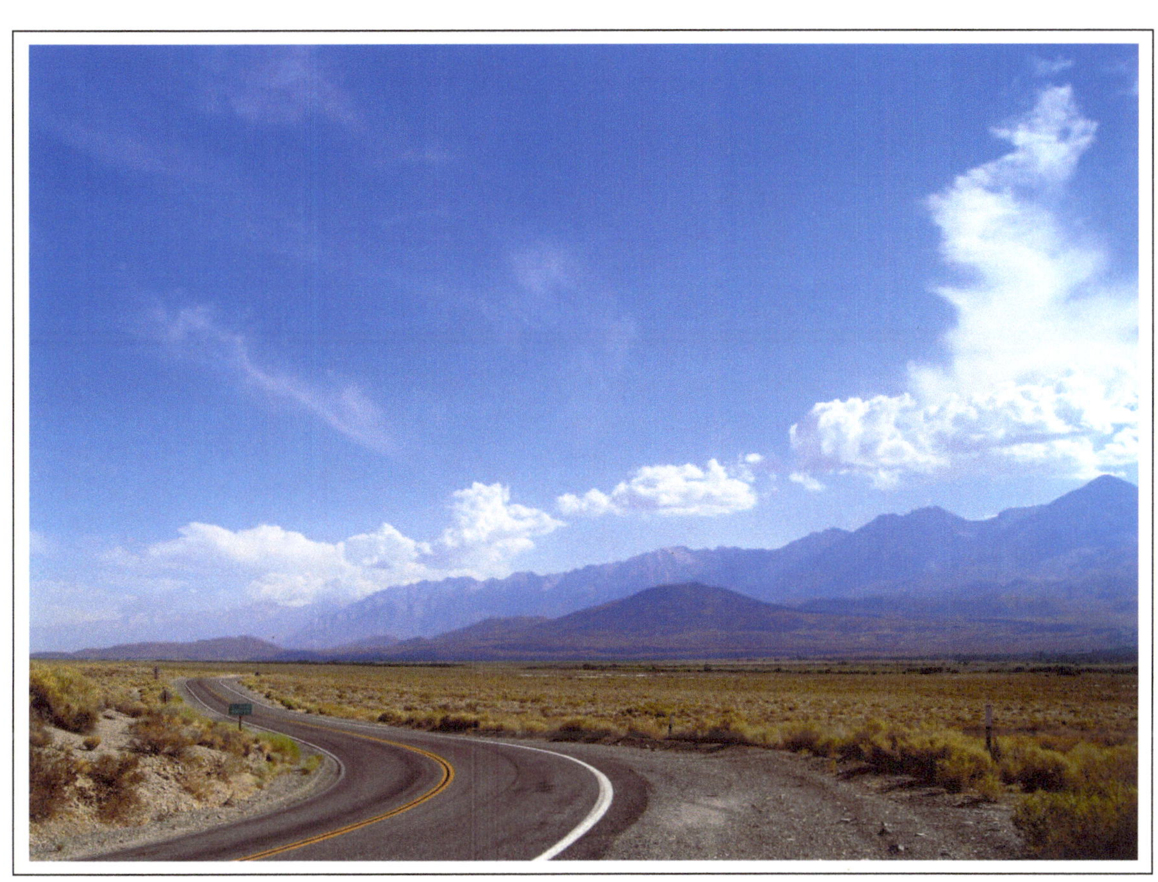

Poetry

Words of poetry
along meandering streams
seep into marshy loam
or melt like chocolate bars
in the light of heaven's dome.

Words well-worn
stop making sense
then spring anew each morn,
reborn in present tense,
then laid to rest each evensong.

Leaping across bouquets
of hovering clouds,
grasping scorching sunrays,
poetry lifts me above the crowds,
towing me along the blue way.

Up I go till I kiss the sky
with outstretched hand
scattering words up high,
then streaming down to the land
like raindrops to beautify.

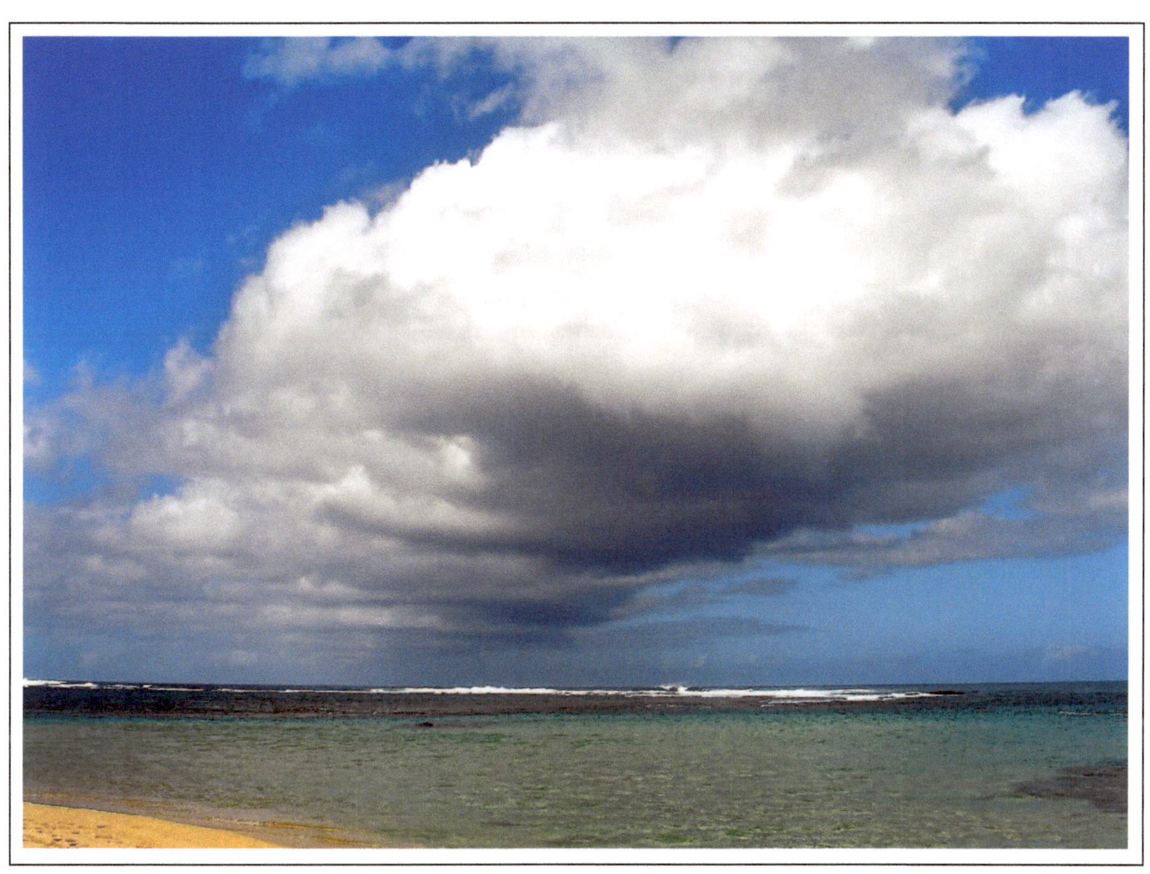

AGAINST SUSPENSION

Strident trumpeting,
tumbling trashcans,
leaves whirling
in updrafts all around.

Inside, silence –
perfect balance
suspended in midair
of captive breath.

Hummingbird hovers
over my unruly hair
bobbing like flowers
with blustery bravado.

Caught in suspension
she flutters and hums,
forever haunting
my life in a trance.

Oh no, push now!
Swell the lungs,
release the breath,
blast the silence!

Against suspension
where all things die
I run to meet
the oncoming wind.

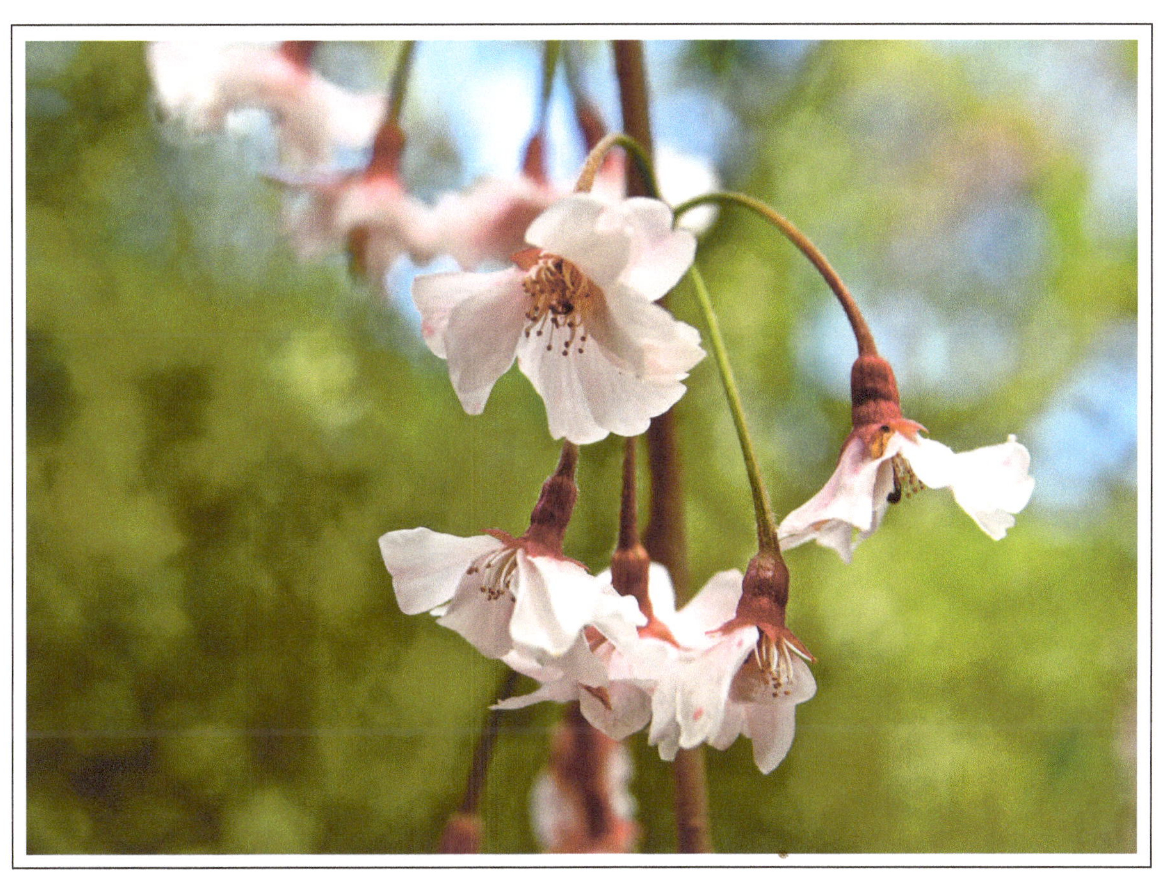

Blithe Is Spirit

I soar and stretch
void my mind
suffices now
to let bliss sunder cells
now when nothing matters
yet matter will matter
for blithe is spirit
and when I descend
I pray the ground
my feet to hold
my hands to sink
into the sand
my hair to twine
with the wind
the ocean to drain
all tears away
for blithe is spirit
and matter will uphold

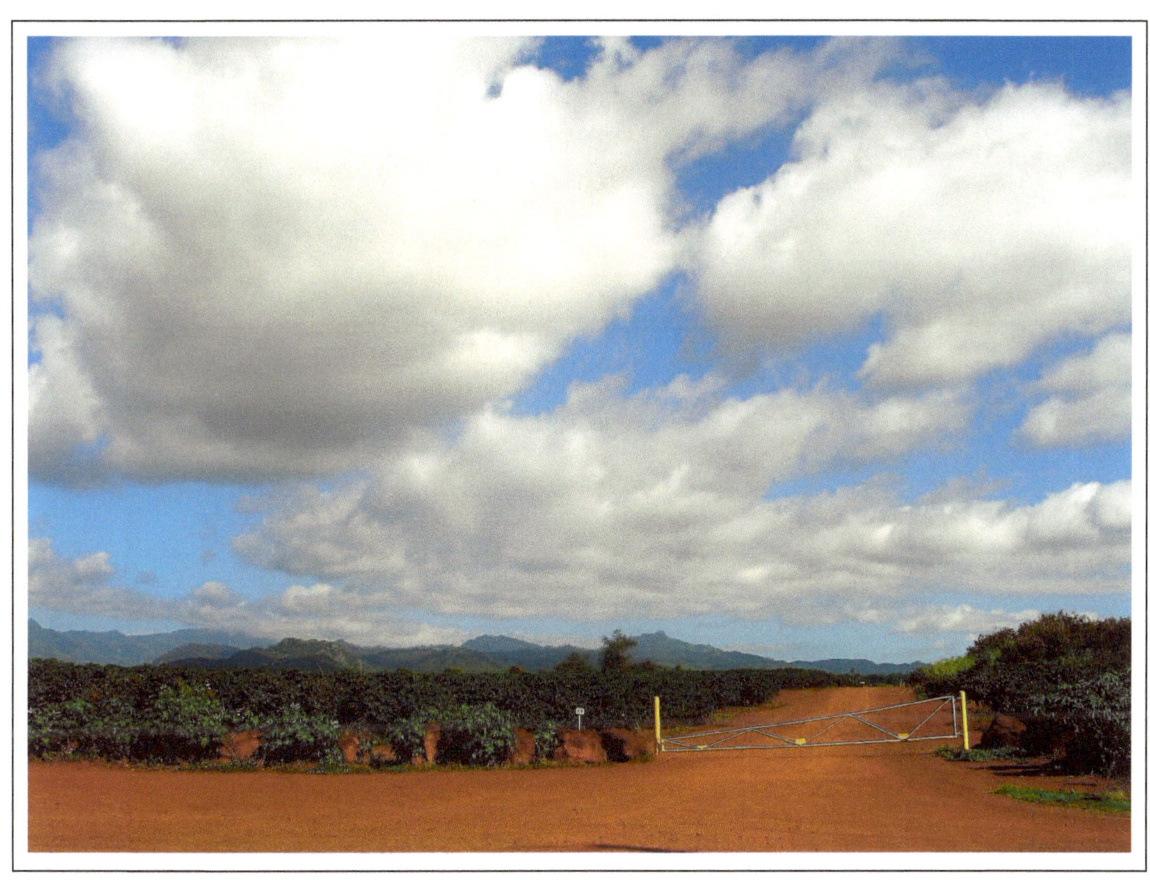

All Traces Of Things

See how the trees
stand bare to the bone
against the sky
of wintry blue,
a cursive testament
that in the end
what remains
are the traces of things,
faded architectural plans
of a once mighty god
now swept away
by the progress of time.
The designer gone,
nothing left of the mind
that started it all,
except the emptiness
of a yawning canvas.
Nothing left but the bare,
bare essence of bones,
like musical notes
on ancient parchments
waiting for rain
to stir up the sap.
In time,
new melodies will rise,
new water flow,
and all traces of things
will sound forth
renewed once more.

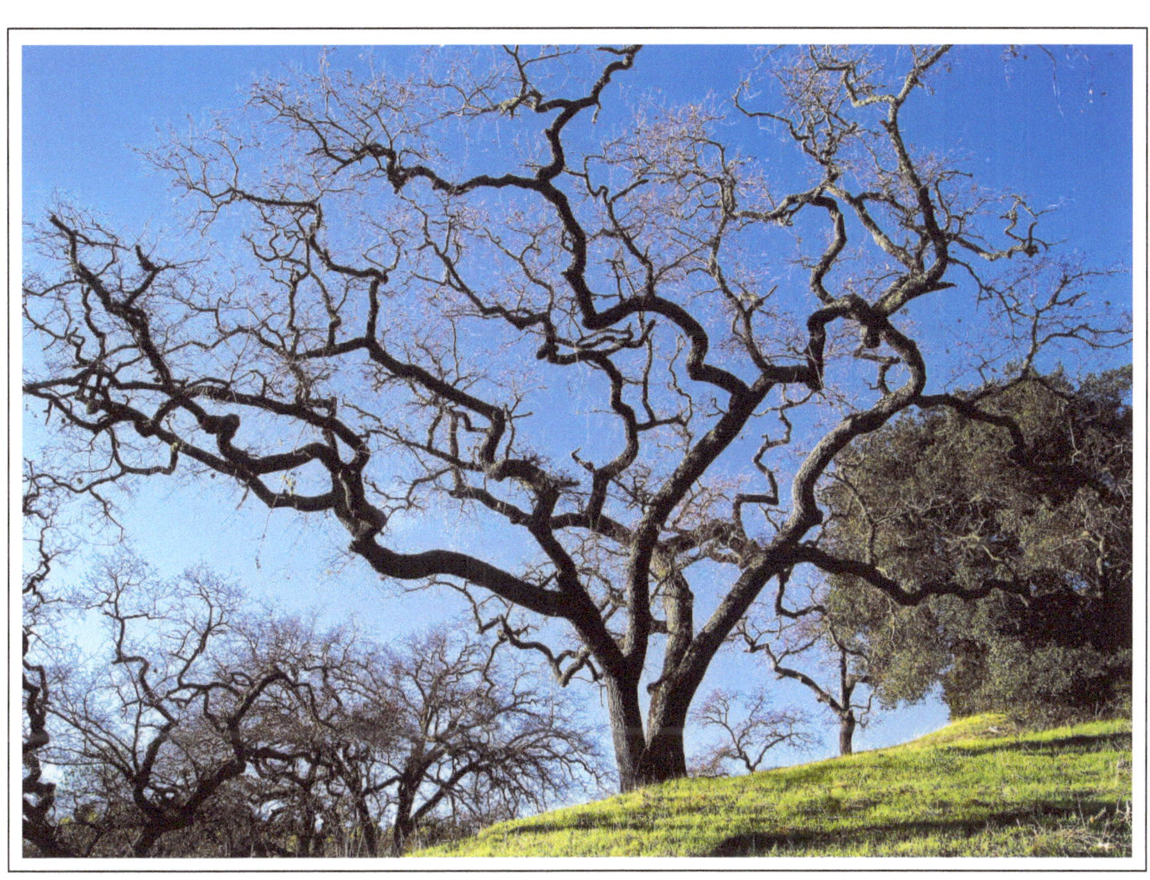

Baptism Of Splendor

Winter rosebud
graced with raindrops
in a bed of dying blooms

in that place
where darts of light
pierce the leaden clouds with flame

cheek to bud
where splendor tilts
she laps the raindrop from my brow

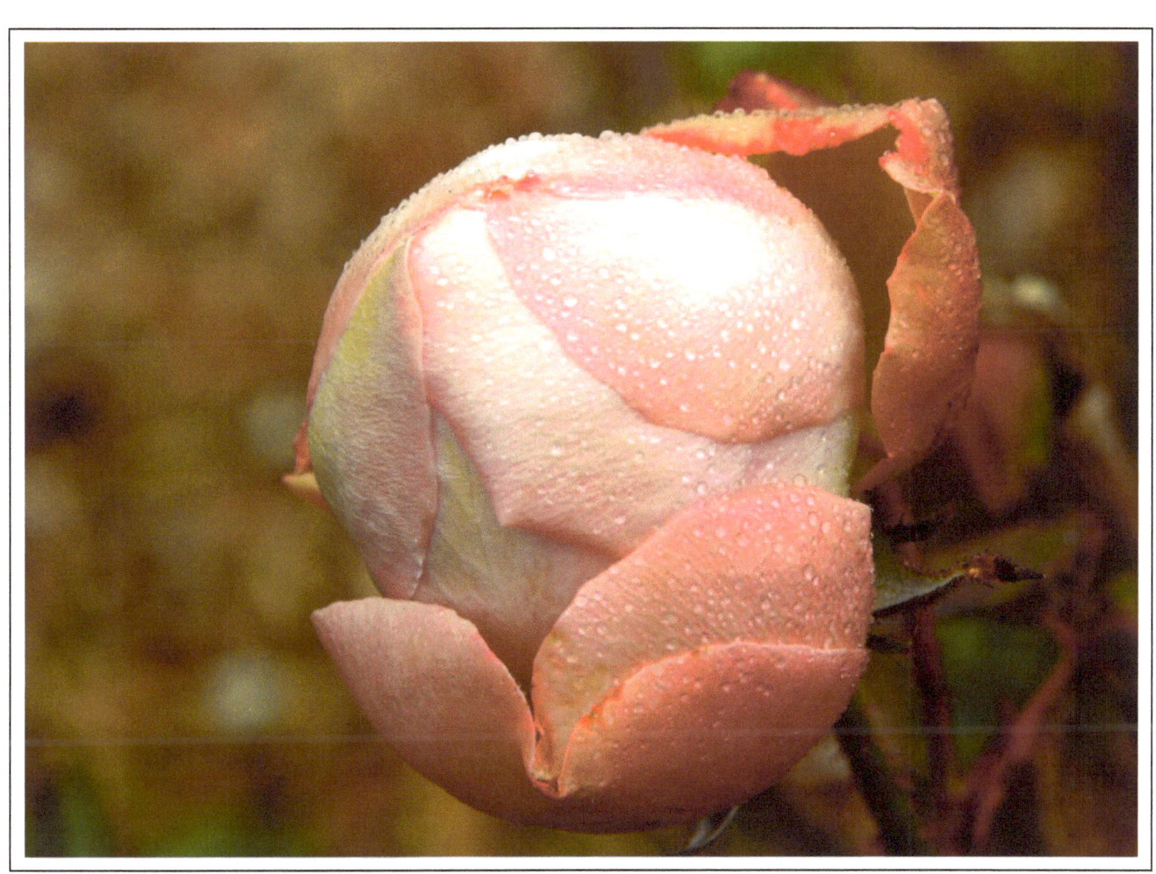

Blue On Blue

Here come the Blue Jays
in feathers of lucid blue.
I expect songs celestial,
but they stun the quiet valleys
with their jarring primal screams.

It is as if Mother Nature,
bored with endless perfection,
dismissed the final brushstroke,
preferring a loony cartoon
to a portrait of utter refinement.

So here I stand scoffing,
yet I drink in all that blue,
blue tipped in velvet blue,
blue traced in blue above,
until I too become all blue.

Now I know what Nature wants:
to topple pomp to earth,
jar complacency with mirth,
and make us doddering lunatics
for her own royal merriment.

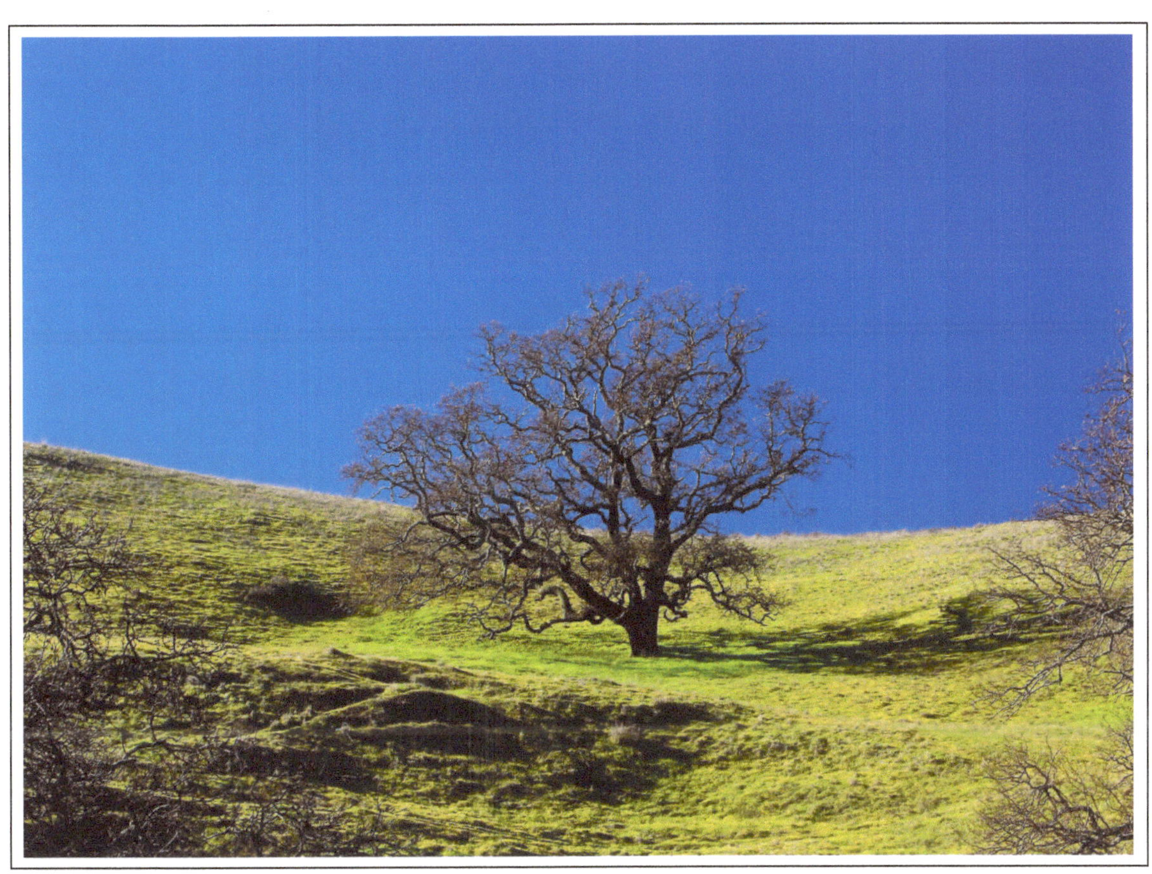

One Petal

Just one petal
in curved suspension,
rosy peach pulsations
along my skin,
carnal perfume
dissolving all sense.

Then my spirit stirs,
for it loves the justness of it,
the oneness of it,
the astonishment of a petal
afloat on a wing of the universe.

If only we knew
that our earth is like this,
a petal from the sun
afloat in the universe,
transcending all sense.
Do you see the frailty of it?
Can you love and care for it?

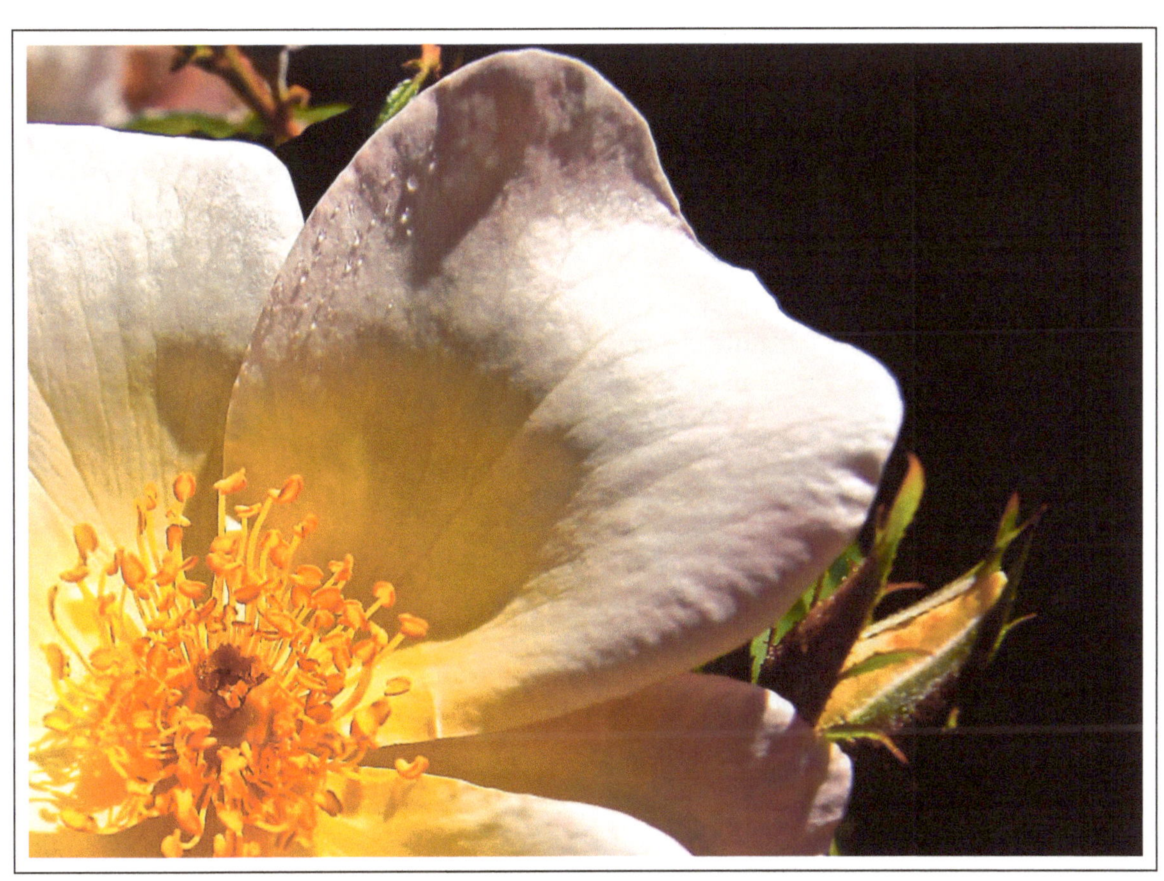

Under Canopy Of Stars

There goes the bumblebee,
frantic and fretting,
mad hatter missing his sup,
like the mad rush of cars
at the close of day,
loudest humming of all.

When does it stop?
Nature designs to keep us puffing,
bumblebees and hoards on wheels.
Take a whiff of that one
heading straight on
to the mother load!

Give me seeds of silence
and I will plant them deep,
deep in the deepest blue,
looking down at the end of day,
then see who is dancing now
in the starlit glow!

Lightness of being
leaves every footprint tilting,
tilting towards the twilight
as we hum incantations
to the canopy of stars
adrift above the din.

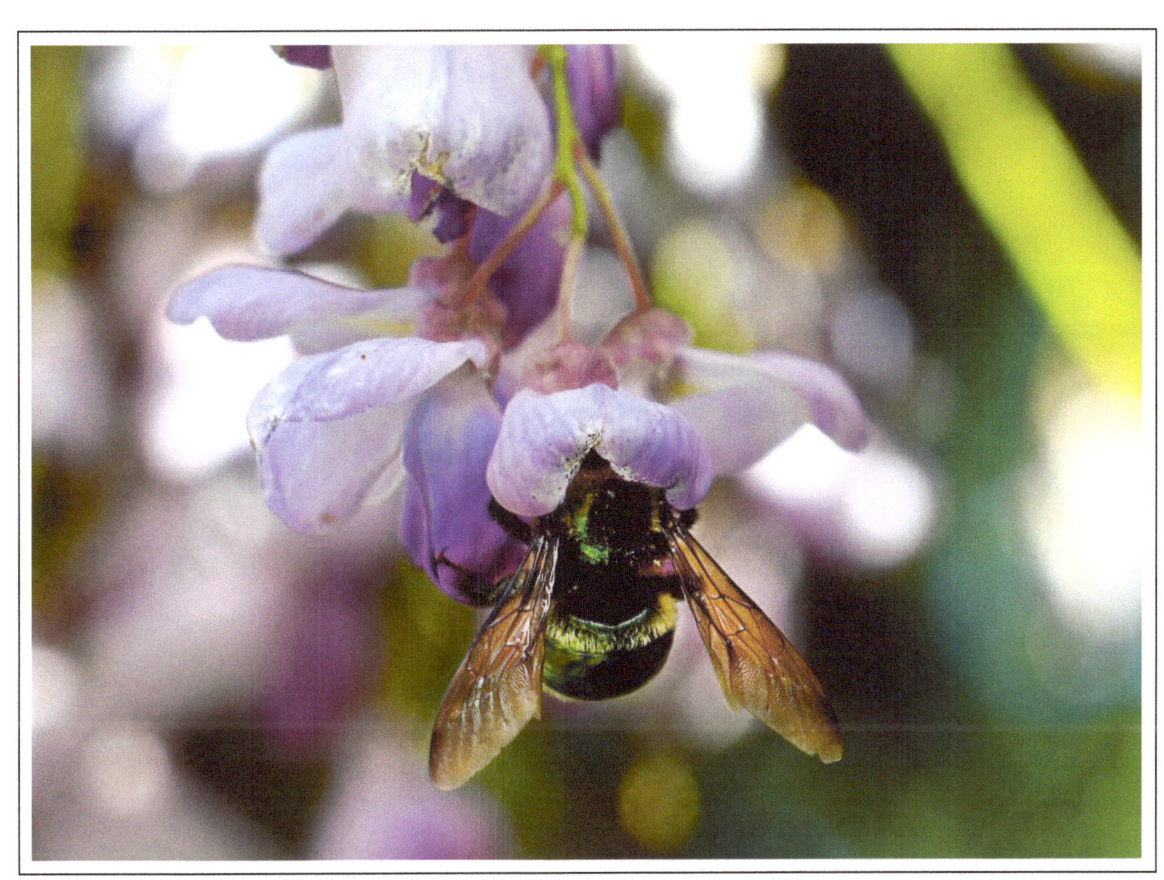

Sky-borne Umbrellas

Senses soothed by sibilant tones,
hummingbirds hovering with ease
and breezes through the leaves.

Bees and bumblebees too,
liquid feast to sky-borne ears
blotting and easing all fears.

Eyes shut I marvel at the hum
invading all my senses,
the land below wafting up incense.

In this billowing ascent
sky-borne umbrellas
cup the rising song a cappella.

It is good to be above the din
where the air is redolent
with fragrant sentiment.

Far below all hustles and bustles,
but here above the hurtling abyss
all that matters is unadorned bliss.

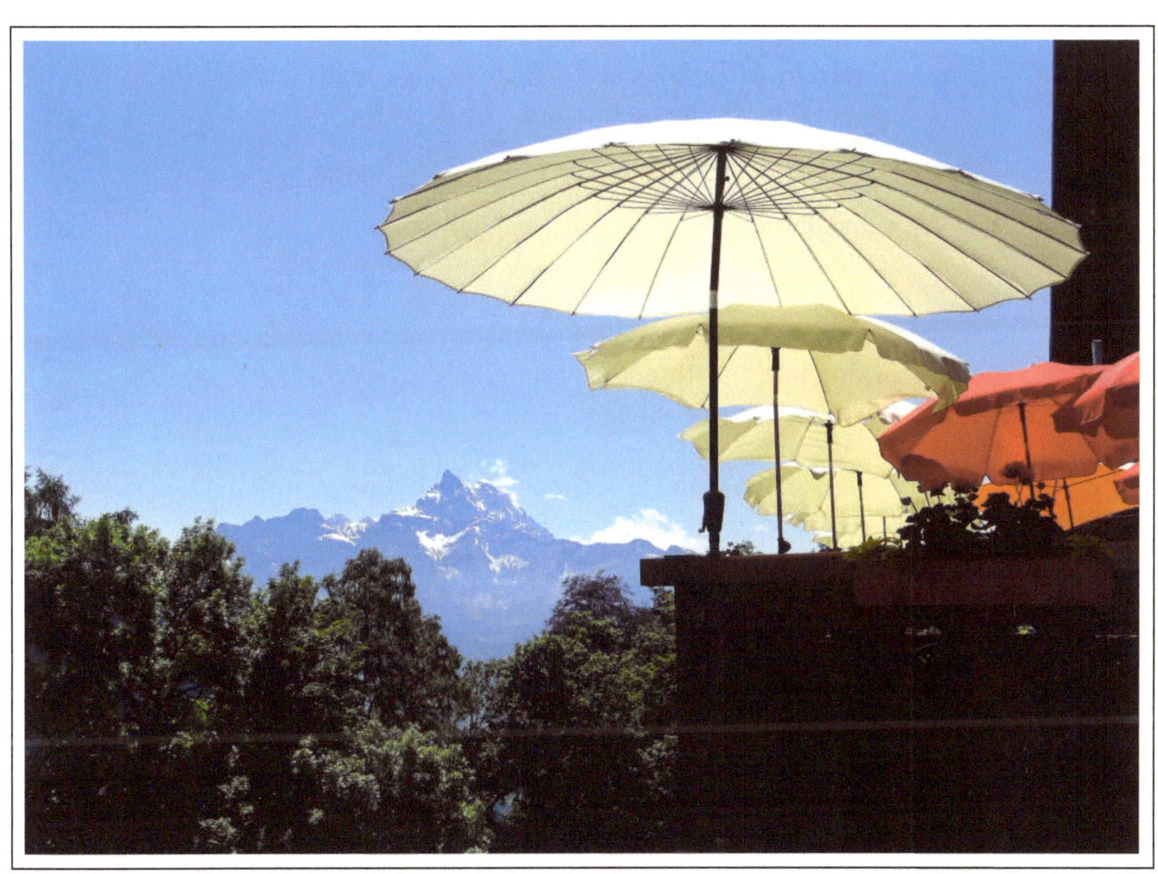

Simplicity All Lit Up

See the shape of the leaf, simplicity all lit up,
formed by earth drenched in a sea-washed glade,
love of life lighting up the forest shade.

The awakened seed rises up through mud,
a bud unfurled waving in the rising flood,
seeking who knows what unseen force of love.

Lean in to the tree trunk, hear the sound
of rhythmic breath not far behind in the breeze
singing songs to the Beloved hidden in the reeds.

See the shape of the leaf, simplicity all lit up.
It was formed by breath pouring into space,
seeking that one elemental breeze to embrace.

Why struggle? You will never know simplicity
until you become the breath resolved into the seas
where the most elemental life is you and the breeze.

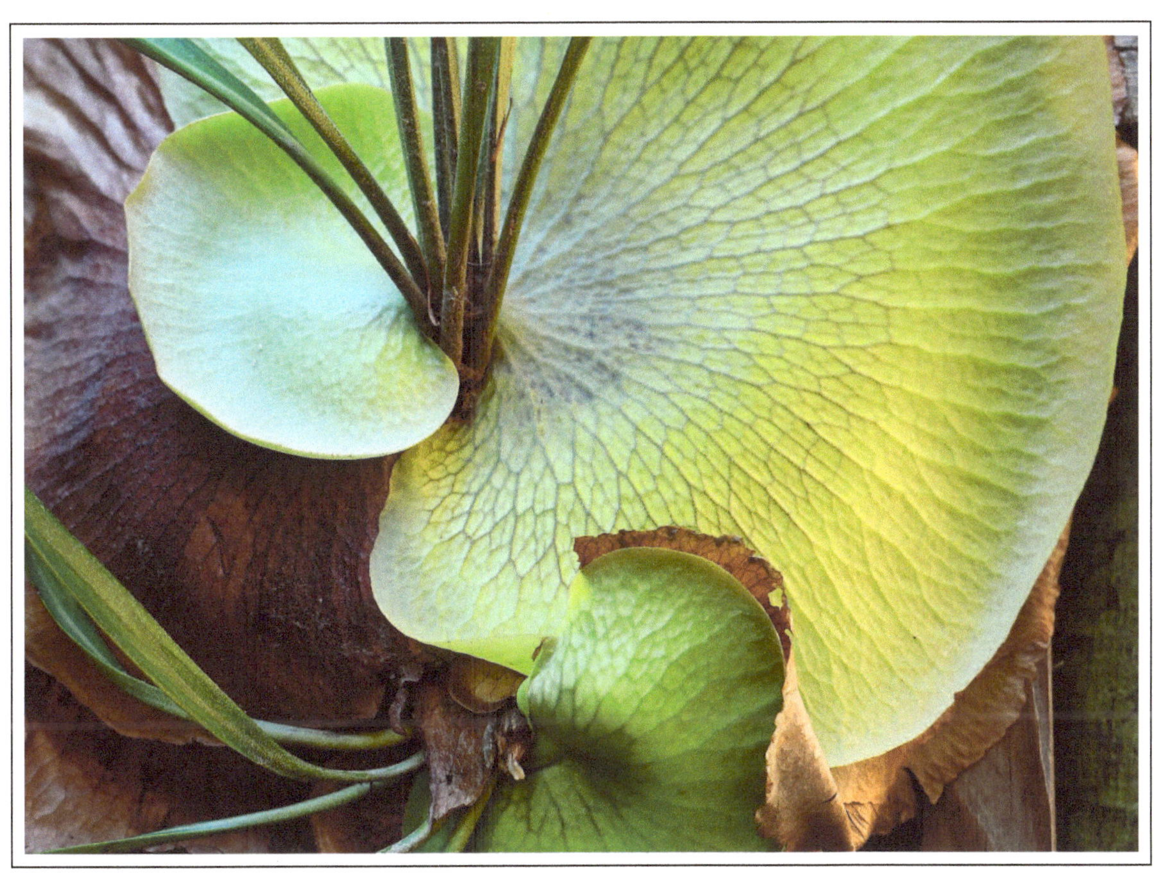

CLARITY IS GIVEN

Everywhere,
beads of splendor
seeding the air with light
so much deeper than the sun,
so much gentler too,
bathing butterflies in the glow,
sheltering petals from the wind.
So it dawns on me now
that clarity is not earned
by just being present here,
but given when we slog
through the suffocating mire.

For clarity is given
at the unexpected hour,
in the deepest bog of doubt
when we cast our eyes above
for a lifeline to the top.
Then clarity is given –
like a soft dusting of the windows,
ducks paddling across the pond,
swallows gliding through reads,
early Spring buds kissing shadows
daubed with beads of splendor,
everywhere.

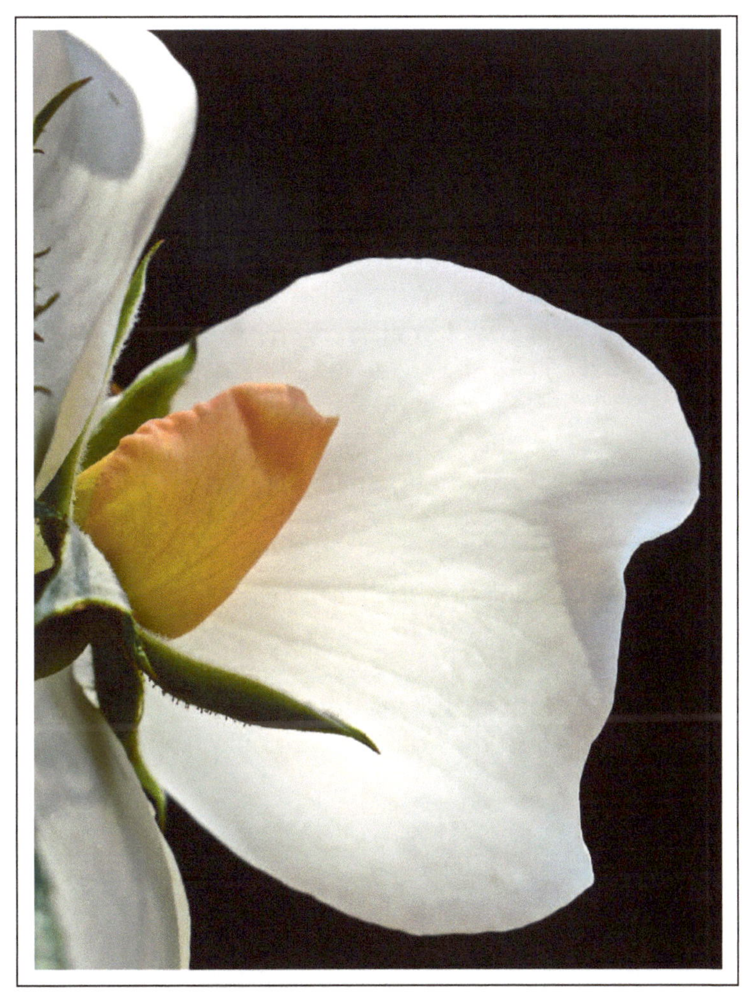

DELICIOUS NOT TO THINK

Delicious not to think,
waves of silence
washing over,
preparing the ground
for a thought surpassing
all the foolish prattling.

I trudge up the hill
tasting dew at every step.
Dark the night
but I know the path so well,
starlit sky
beacon to my stilled mind.

Delicious not to think
when the moon is at rest,
stars abloom
in liquid sky,
lotuses dipping down
over the brimming ground.

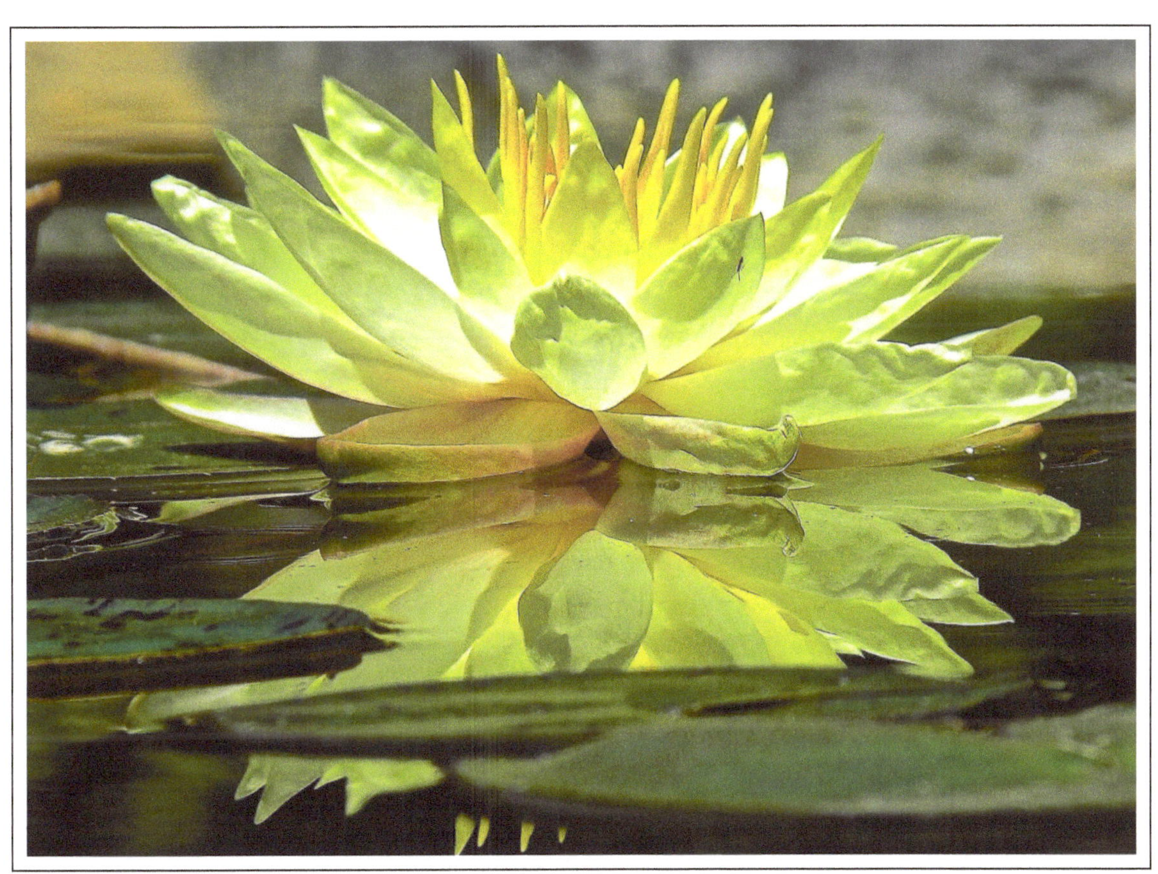

STILLNESS IS NOT SILENCE

When silence descends,
I sink into the sound of stillness,
the symphony of all symphonies,
the universal hum,
God's voice holding me aloft.

Can you hear it?
Behind chatter, behind thought,
along that deep highway
from the seat of your being
to the height of your longing,
from lotus to crown,
ladder to heaven,
feeding your blood
from toe nails to hair tips.

Can you hear it?
The sonorous trace of a harp string,
the soothing sibilance of a singing reed,
the long wail of the Coltrane sax,
still reverberating in his passing.
Birds hold the fullness of it,
fly with it, mate with it,
until their chests below forth
their coda to the waiting God.

Stillness is not silence,
it is the hum of life,
surging through you in the song of you,
God's ears thrilling with you,
swaying with you in the forest clearing.

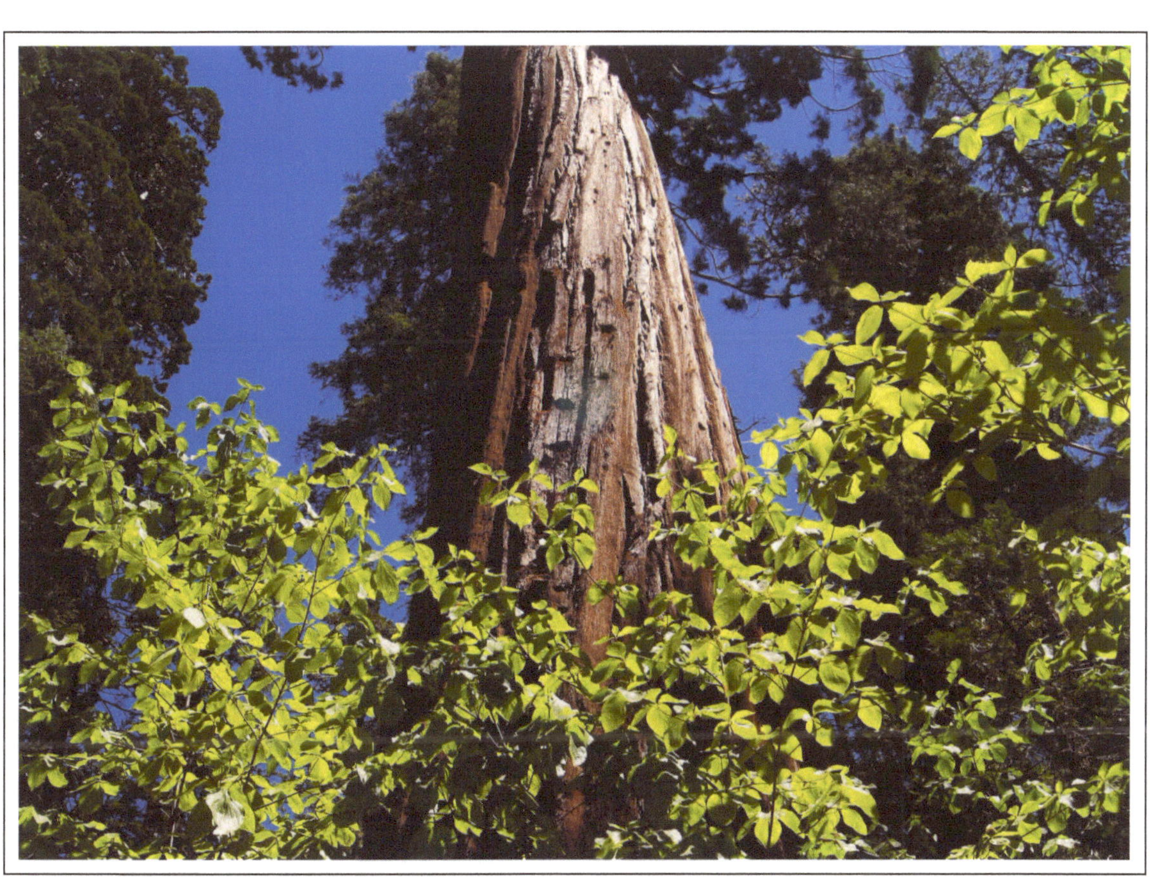

Butterfly In A Frame

Butterfly in a frame,
fluttering but not seen,
as I wait for words to flow,
but oh so ponderous and slow.

Little does she know
how I framed her for all time,
mesmerized by the blush
of that flower oh so lush.

Waiting now for words,
something shifts deep inside,
there where the heart aflame
lights up the sleeping brain.

I meet the rising flutter
along the ridges of my mind,
spilling forth in living color
all the pent up flaming ardor.

Butterfly in my frame,
now I see you each day
as a yearning to rise and say
the words of freedom's way.

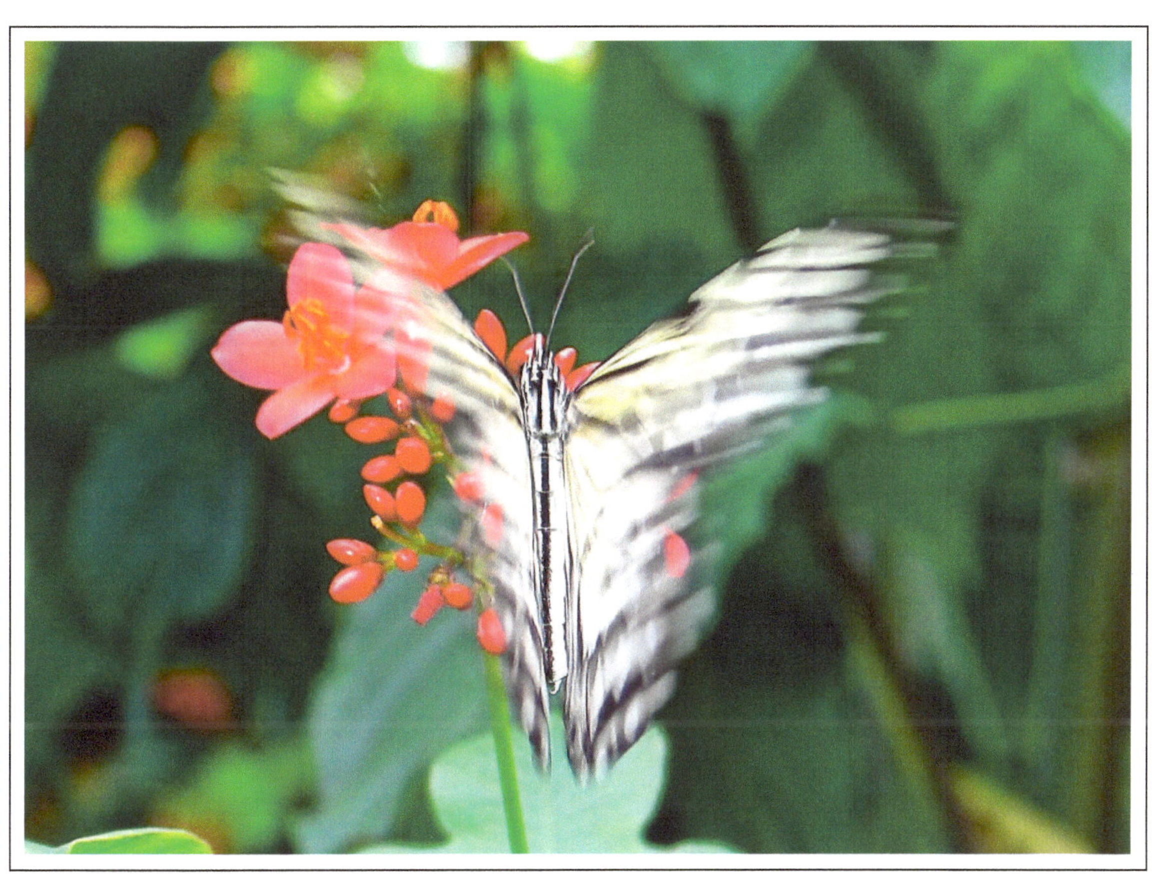

EPILOGUE: BROWN

Some years ago my brown bird muse came and sang to me, changing my view of the world. Now my muse has become many and I have learned to distinguish their myriad shades of brown and sonorous sounds.

Brown: who would have thought that humble earth-bound brown could hold such richness of tone, from ashen earth to the burnished glow of sunlight to the glossy brown tinged with the blackness of night.

If nothing comes to fill the blank canvas of my mind, I open my senses to the fluttering of the muses – browning and toning my mind. If I stumble in the glamour of big words, I reach for brown, anchoring me to the bedrock of humble beginnings.

"Keep it simple," chirp the muses,
"keep it simple and join our song,
keep it simple and you can't go wrong."

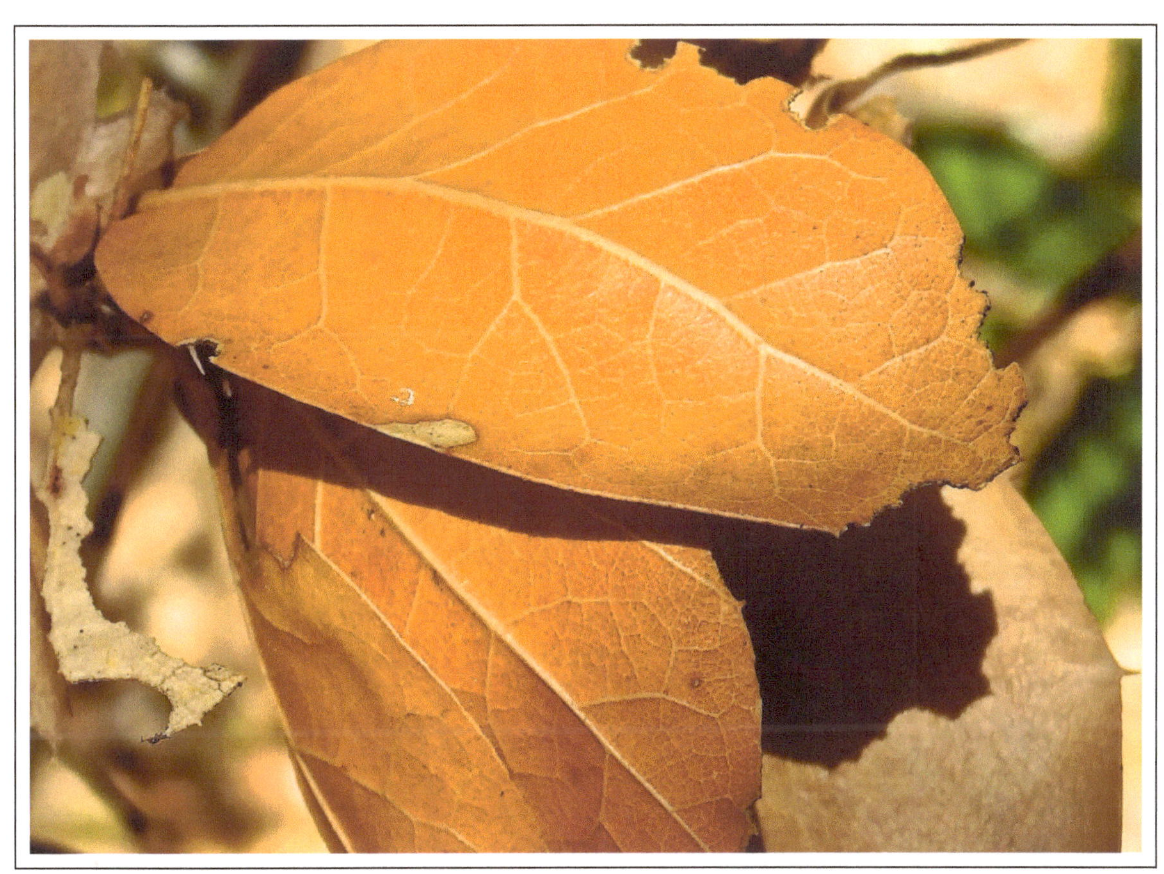

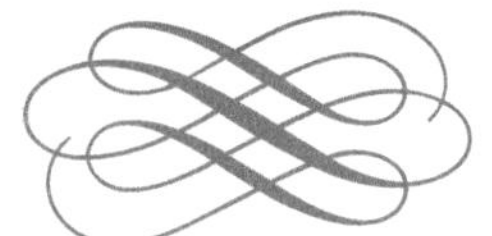

Photography Index

Page 39: Dahlia in the Light: Filoli, Woodside, CA, August 2013.

Page 41: The New Vine: Limantour Beach, Pt. Reyes, CA, March 2010.

Page 43: Part II, Leaning on Love: Sutter Creek Inn, Sutter Creek, CA, April 2014

Page 45: Grandma's Iron Stove: El Chile, Honduras, March 2005.

Page 47: Ancestral Boars and Bovines: Shenandoah Valley, Amador County, CA, April 2014.

Page 49: Coyote Friend: Mt. Burdell, Novato, CA, March 2013.

Page 51: When Winter Comes: Jack London House of Happy Walls Museum, Glen Ellen, November 2010.

Page 53: Tall Grasses: Atherton Pond, Novato, June 2005.

Page 55: Maybe You: Genessee, Idaho, April 2010.

Page 57: The Line: Mt. Burdell, Novato, CA, March 2013.

Page 59: On Dying in Love: St. Prex, Switzerland, July 2013.

Page 61: Desire: Olympic National Park, WA, June 2007; Yosemite National Park, CA, April 2006; Limantour Beach, Point Reyes, CA, March 2010.

Page 63: Canticle: University of California Botanical Gardens, Berkeley, CA, January 2011.

Page 65: On Seeing Love: Ancient Bristlecone Pine Forest, White Mountains, Inyo County, CA, August 2012.

Page 97: One Petal: Filoli, Woodside, CA, August 2013.

Page 99: Under Canopy of Stars: Sutter Creek Inn, Sutter Creek, CA, April 2014.

Page 101: Sky-borne Umbrellas: Gryon, Aigle, Canton of Vaud, Switzerland, July 2013.

Page 103: Simplicity All Lit Up: From a private garden in San Rafael, CA, March 2014.

Page 105: Clarity is Given: Filoli, Woodside, CA, August 2014.

Page 107: Delicious not to Think: The Gamble House, Pasadena, CA, June 2010.

Page 109: Stillness is not Silence: Stanislaus National Forest, Sonora, CA, July 2012.

Page 111: Butterfly in a Frame: The Burtchart Gardens, Victoria, BC, June 2007.

Page 113: Brown: Mt. Burdell, Novato, CA, December 2013.

Back Cover: More Flying Berries, Atherton Trail, Novato, CA, August 2013.

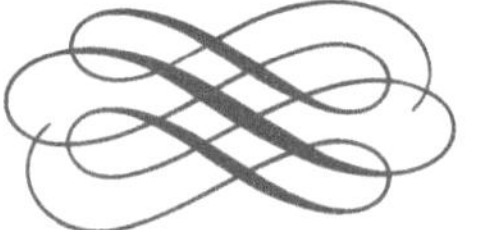

About the Author

Cristina Olsen, PhD, received her Masters in Philosophy and Religion from the California Institute of Integral Studies and her Doctorate in Spirituality and Cultural Geography from the Graduate Theological Union in Berkeley, California. She is the author of *Nature in the Lives of Saints Brigit, Patrick and Columba*, Lambert Academic Publishing, Saarbrucken, Germany, 2012. She has taught courses in world religions, nature mysticism, and meditative practices at various institutions throughout the Bay Area, and has lectured in the United States, England, Wales and Scotland on topics in Celtic Spirituality and nature mysticism. In addition, she raised funds for nonprofit institutions in the area of environmental education, sustainable agriculture in rural communities in Africa, Asia, and Central and South America, interfaith dialogue, hospice care, and higher education. Born in Argentina, Cristina also worked as an English teacher and a Spanish-English translator in Argentina and Chile. Cristina is a lifelong student of Archetypal Psychology and is a member of the C.G. Jung Institute in San Francisco. She lives in Marin County with her husband, fellow poet and photographer, Dave Muñoz (Haiku Dave), and has a small private practice as a Certified Creative Writer and Publishing Coach.

Special thanks to my book designer Jim Shubin.
You bring out the elegance buried deep in everything.
This is your book too.

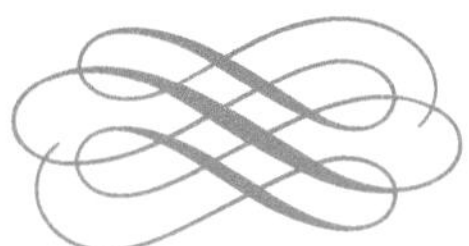

www.ingramcontent.com/pod-product-compliance
Lightning Source LLC
Chambersburg PA
CBHW042148030726
47599CB00004B/656